Robert Harbinson was born in Belfast in 1928 and he was educated there and in Enniskillen, Co. Fermanagh. He worked for a short time as a cabin boy on a dredger in Belfast Lough, then started training as a medical missionary. He left Belfast in 1944 to study theology at the South Wales Bible College and he went on to teach in north Devon, Canada and Venezuela. He took up diamond prospecting in Canada and South America and his hunting and trapping with the Blackfoot and Stony Indians began a long interest in American Indians who feature in his many travel books which were published in the 1960s under the name of Robin Bryans.

In more recent years he has become involved in music, concentrating on his work as an opera librettist from his London home/music studio.

No Surrender is the first volume of his four-part autobiography which continues with *Up Spake the Cabin Boy, Song of Erne* and *The Protégé*. In addition to these and his travel books he has also published *Tattoo Lily and Other Ulster Stories,* the novel *Lucio,* and his collection of poems *Songs Out of Oriel.*

NO SURRENDER

An Ulster Childhood

by
**ROBERT
HARBINSON**

**THE
BLACKSTAFF
PRESS**

First published in 1960 by
Faber and Faber Limited
This Blackstaff Press edition is a photolithographic facsimile
of the second edition printed by Latimer Trend & Co. Limited

This edition published in 1987 by
The Blackstaff Press Limited
3 Galway Park, Dundonald, Belfast BT16 0AN, Northern Ireland
with the assistance of
The Arts Council of Northern Ireland

Reprinted 1988, 1989

Printed in Northern Ireland by
The Universities Press Limited

British Library Cataloguing in Publication Data
Harbinson, Robert
No surrender: an Ulster childhood. —
3rd ed.
1. Northern Ireland — Social life and
customs
1. Title
941.6082'2'0924   DA990.46
ISBN 0-85640-383-0

For

BIG 'INA

Optimam Matrem

Contents

Local Terms

Allan Hawk	Red-throated Diver
Blaeberry	Bilberry
Black-mouths	Presbyterians
Boxty	Potato Cake
Buckie-berries	Wild Rose Seeds
Crane	Heron
Fenians	Roman Catholics
French-fuzz	Gorse
God's Goat	Snipe
Half-moons	Goldcrests
Jack-in-the-box	Lords and Ladies
Jenny Dabbers	Common Terns
Jinny	Effeminate Person
King Billy	William III
Lady's Thimble	Harebell
Mackerel Cock	Manx Shearwater
Make	Halfpenny
Marleys	Marbles
Mickeys	Roman Catholics
Mitch School	Play Truant
Moss-cheeper	Meadow Pipit
Mudlark	Dunlin
Piss-a-bed	Dandelion
Pollen	Fresh Water Herring

11

Local Terms

Purple Charlies	Early Purple Orchids
Reeler	Nightjar
Robin-run-the-hedge	Larger Bindweed
Scabby-gub	Hemlock
Shin-hates	Sitting by Fire
Snapping Lads	Himalayan Balsam
Snaw Cock	Mistle Thrush
Spricks	Minnows
Steepwort	Butterwort
Whaap	Curlew
Wing	Penny
Yellow Yorling	Yellowhammer

Spit of the Ould Da

There are no more weavers in Ballymacarrett.

Now, when the blasting lay-off siren wails above the screeching din of hammers and pneumatic riveters, the shipyard gates open. Into the dirty streets of the once quiet townland swarm the grimy workers. Pavements teem with youths and gaunt fathers, the air smells of a day's work, its grease and sweat. Hurrying with an unnatural speed, everyone is anxious only to get home to the kitchen sink and remove the stigma of toil. Afterwards, transformed, there could be a visit to the dogs, a session over pots of porter, or a game of marleys.

Big 'Ina heard *the Albert* strike four o'clock on a warm spring afternoon. Because of the great load that sagged heavily under her pinny, the air seemed oppressive. She felt hot and bothered, and thought of an ice from Leo's ice-cream parlour down the street. Before the men came spewing out from the yard there would be time to get a penny wafer. It did her good, so much good, that she decided to spend a second wing on another. And as she was licking it, a sharp pain gripped her and she realized the time had come to get Nurse Calvert. But barely had Big 'Ina got inside the door when I made my entry into the world.

The event was spectacular. Nearly eleven pounds I weighed. 'Ya've the muscles of a man,' said the district nurse when she congratulated Big 'Ina on having such a brute. My mother

13

never forgot the nurse's remark. The years that followed were to prove that only those muscles would ensure our survival.

Not that the event shook the world—it had other things to think about. The gay twenties were coming to an end. On that very day Mr. Churchill introduced his budget, a tax on imported buttons, and a farthing off sugar. The Duke of Gloucester took his seat in the House of Lords, and another titled gentleman was arrested in Hyde Park when trying to share his seat with a lady of the town. Gay—but not for everyone. In Greece an earthquake rocked Corinth, a plague of locusts appeared on the shores of Galilee, and a hungry brat sought for Big 'Ina's breast. But for the small house in Ballymacarrett, the world was the baby.

When the young sire came down the street, ladder over shoulder with his bucket swinging from the end, Cissy, the first-born, ran to tell him the news. He bolted up the stairs and snatched up the purple-faced bundle. The squalling thing fulfilled his dearest wish of a son, and of course, it would be called Robbie after him. The excitement, localized in the dockside house, did not even reach as far as the clergy of the parish church. They, whose business was to disseminate hope and joy in our close streets, saw so many offspring coming into a hopeless and joyless world, and had become indifferent. Big 'Ina could wait, no rector was going to the house for *her* baby. When sufficient names crowded the list—a fortnight later—I was carried off to the big church round the corner that heaved its Victorian gothic bulk above the mean dock houses.

That night many babies awaited baptism, and the curate was in a hurry to get started. Perhaps the church had chilled since the day's heat, perhaps his supper lay ready, perhaps despair at the despair of our world gnawed his soul. Anyway, I joined the first queue of my life, and so came into the heritage of the poor. Aunt Dottie, a cousin of my mother's, acted as my only godparent.

Spit of the Ould Da

In Aunt Dottie's view Big 'Ina had 'come down' in the world by marrying my father, for their side of the family was comparatively well-to-do. My mother's parents both died and she was farmed out to an aunt who resented her intrusion. At the age of twelve Big 'Ina, properly called Georgina, went to work in the mill. Those muscles of which the nurse spoke, formed young. Though callous, the relatives maintained sufficient interest to oppose her marriage vigorously. In their opinion, the man she wanted was beneath her, and a reputation for wildness and an over-fondness of the bottle did not help. But in defiance, Big 'Ina and Robbie joined a church queue and got married, *en masse* with seventeen other couples. Afterwards they went off on a two-shilling excursion to Bangor and had a grand high tea at a Mrs. McGowan's boarding-house, before returning to Ballymacarrett to start breeding.

When the aunts kept away, my father worked well enough and was popular with everyone whose windows he cleaned.

We left Ballymacarrett when I reached the age of five months, an age when I had already contracted a shipyard bark, the result, people thought, of the bronchitis that lingered about my young chest. My paternal grandfather died and left us his house on the other side of the city. It was rented, and though valued at no more than a hundred pounds, during the years that ensued we paid upwards of a thousand pounds for the scruffy little house, in coins so indignantly demanded every Monday morning by the rent clerk.

People considered the new house smart for it boasted two bedrooms and a return, though it is true only tiny ones. It stood so close to the railway that the whole structure shook from the foundations, day and night, from the passing trains. Out of the front bedroom where we all huddled together in the big brass bed, the window gave a view across a roof wilderness of near-slums whose only contact with heaven was by belching chimney-stacks that fingered the sky. It was to be the scene of my childhood until I was twelve. Bliss and tragedy were to fall on Big 'Ina's baby scarcely half a year old then. Later, he looked back on those years as the most wonderful of his life.

But the rows of houses did not go on for ever. Beyond them lay the Bog Meadows' marshy steppes where refuse heaps broke the flatness, and where the narrow, shallow Blackstaff River meandered, colourless and unmusical. Near its banks the tinkers camped. We at least held hopes in our heart—who knew, one day we might even have the chance of a council house. But the tinkers could not warm themselves with such a comfort but only over reluctant fires that hissed in the drizzle outside their tents of rags.

God ordained that even the Bog Meadows should end and had set a great hill at their limit, which we called the Mickeys' Mountain. Among a knot of trees half-way up the flank a small cottage sheltered, and near by two fields were cultivated. Seen from the Bog Meadows they stood out amongst the bracken and heather like a giant hatchet. In terms of miles the mountain was not far, and I always longed to explore it. Somewhere, or in the hidden hills behind, lay the boot stuffed with goldpieces buried by Neeshy Haughan, who once upon a time robbed the rich to pay the poor, kindnesses ended by a hanging at Carrickfergus. What things might be bought with the highwayman's long boot of gold! But the mountain was inaccessible because to reach it we had to cross territory held by the Mickeys. Being children of the staunch Protestant quarter, to go near the Catholic idolators was more than we dared, for fear of having one of our members cut off.

I settled early on rebel dreams. My father was too much like Neeshy Haughan, wild and free. My life became embedded in his and I rushed to his defence whenever people attacked him on account of his wildness. Soon, when I grew to be five years

16

old, tragedy struck at us. Playing with the tinker children in the Bog Meadows one day, I found some whitethorn blossom, and thinking to delight my mother, took it home. She recognized the evil omen and threw the blossom out. But it was too late. Before nightfall the hospital call came—Big 'Ina's fella had fallen from the top window of a house in the rich suburbs and broken his limbs. His head was spiked on the railings, his brain fatally damaged. He was twenty-seven years old, his wild music sung, his passion cased in plaster of Paris.

Then began the terrible days which have chased me down the long corridors of life ever since. For months he lay on the horsehair sofa in the kitchen, delirious in body and mind. I can see him now, unable to join us in the brass bed, lying amid the bandages, and covered by his father's old lamp-lighter's greatcoat. He always wanted his melodeon near, though he could play it no more. And in my last memory of him, I see him on the sofa, where sometimes I would find odd coins that had rolled down the side. It was Christmas Eve, and my mother had gone to see my younger sister who had scarlet fever. Looking up I saw tears rolling down the unshaven face. I thought maybe he was sorry for having filled the house with vast terror earlier in the day, when my mother went near to wash him. Or perhaps his soul was fighting to be out in the Bog Meadows with his red-setter bitch, or playing his melodeon on the quayside as the emigrant boats sailed out from the harbour. Perhaps he wept because he realized that life was almost over, and he must leave the boys on the corner, the pigeons on the mangle in the backyard, the tin porringer of whelks from the Friday market and the little house in our row.

And so it was.

He never got free of the imprisoning plaster to go down to see friends off to America, his melodeon wheezing out 'God be with you till we meet again', or a good Orange bleat of

'Sons whose sires with William bled'. Before springtime
came again he was taken, we thought, to hospital. Then one
morning a sparrow flew down the parlour chimney and my
mother knew the end had come. And sure enough the same
day my father died.

We had an old saying, 'Happy is the bride the sun shines
on; happy is the corpse the rain rains on.' Undoubtedly it
meant happiness to him that his wrecked body, undermined
by tuberculosis and the effects of hard drinking, to say
nothing of smashed limbs and severed brain, could now rest.
A thunderstorm swept across the city as he was taken very
quietly away. I sat at the great-aunts', cloistered with Bible
story-books and an apple tart with six red candles because it
was my birthday. But as the flails of rain lashed the windows
I thought of the day's events. I had seen my mother borrow
black stockings from next door, and knew why, dressed in
the unusual clothes, she had taken us over to be at the great-
aunts' until all was over. On my jersey sleeve, a diamond-
shaped black patch had been sewn, and my fingers wandered
to pull and fidget the material. While the funeral was taking
place somebody robbed our house. The window-cleaner's
last possession, his ladder, disappeared. The neighbours rightly
said that 'Poor Robbie went without a shammy to his
name.'

Some days after, when we were all at home in our own
house again, a relative brought what we called the 'grave-
papers'. My mother put them in the marble-topped washstand upstairs along with the birth certificates and other
family documents. I was told, as if I ought to know, that the
family grave would now only hold one more adult, alternatively two of us children might be squeezed in.

Time, the unreckoned time of the young, swallowed our
tragedy. Then I started school. The gloomy building and its
dull chores did not interest me much, and after a taunting

remark by my teacher, they became a special hate. The
teacher, a great female Wolsey with triple chins and stomachs,
was called the Tit Queen, a title awarded her on account of
a most enormous bosom. One morning in the playground,
my skylarking roused her wrath, and she resorted to sarcasm,
and made the fatal remark, 'You're as mad as your father
ever was.'

Some finely tensioned cord in me snapped. From then on
I hated her, and all she represented, and became a rebel, very
much with a cause. For years the taunt shadowed my life.
The bitter words haunted me when, later, I got to know
definitely that the 'hospital' had been a mental one, and succeeded in reading the death certificate's dread pronounce-
ment, 'Cause of Death, General Paralysis of the Insane. In-
definite Certified.' How bare of humane feeling could offi-
cialdom be? The long, crisp certificate bore no mention of a
young window-cleaner having an accident; did not even
carry the merciful medical terminology to deaden the pain
for the widow, still little more than a girl; not a thought did
that bald piece of paper spare for the children who wanted
him to come home, and rock them back and forth on his
knee while singing:

> *The Bangor boat's away*
> *We've got no time to stay,*
> *So put on your coat,*
> *And run like a goat,*
> *The Bangor boat's away.*

The memory of my father devoured me. Growing up did
not separate me from him, for in doing so I grew to be like
him. Everyone said, 'You're the spit of your ould da.' The
loathed great-aunts employed this as a scornful term, and they
did not only mean my facial structure which increasingly re-

Spit of the Ould Da

sembled his. But their contempt could be fought by spending long hours in the cemetery, an activity they considered unhealthy.

But I knew that ordinary people regarded my father highly. 'Ordinary people' meant those whose hearts had not shrivelled, and whose emotions were not bottled in vinegar, and who had not got the money and killing respectability of the great-aunts. It pleased me immensely when an ordinary person recognized me as 'Robbie's wee craytur' or when I heard them talking and agreeing that my father had been a 'quare civil fella'. A grain of comfort for my mother came from the doctor who saw him die. Often she told us, I suppose because there was no one else to tell, of the doctor's remark. She repeated with sad wonder that at the end, 'Robbie was like a lad of sixteen.' In death, the lines of anguish and suffering had been smoothed out. Nevertheless, the dashing youth with a cloth cap set at a cocky angle, his pockets full of rhubarb-rock, would come down the street no more to his small world—the world of the big brass bed and the children's lips like split roses that watered as he put hand to pocket.

Snow fell on the first occasion that my two sisters and I were taken to the cemetery by Big 'Ina. We were almost too small to keep pace as she hurried over the eddying, powdered snow to put a holly wreath on the still-new grave. Before we reached it, a melancholy bell tolled the closing time, so we began running. My younger sister was crying and I was afraid the gate would close too soon, and we would have to spend the night with the endless tombstones, the gargantuan angels and sarcophagi, and the cypresses looming out of the whirling flakes. But at last we reached the grave and my mother, leaning over the snow-covered knobbly earth, laid the ring of tough, shiny leaves, and we half-ran, half-walked back to the gates. We were the last out, and the man was cross for being kept late on Christmas Eve. Breathless from running, we passed under the weird street-lamps, our cheeks so hot that the snowflakes melted on touching them.

Working to provide for us through fourteen hours a day, seven days in the week, left my mother no time to go back to the cemetery, but the little plot had a willing guardian in me. Not that death was strange to me, for it often brooded in our streets, with wide bows of black taffeta tied to the knockers, blinds drawn for three days, and the collecting of pennies for wreaths of wax-paper flowers. The shining funeral horses, with froth dripping from their mouths, passed our house on their way home after a day's work, leaving a harvest of golden piles, which were quickly shovelled up for the orange lilies in the window-boxes. I was still a toddler when a small friend took me into the parlour where his grandmother was 'set out'. Because I had been a favourite of the old lady, he pulled the veil back from the coffin and told me I could have a last kiss.

In our own house we had a christening veil. As my face was very pale and unhealthy, hollowed by cavernous cheeks, and I knew nobody expected me to live long, I would dress up in a nightgown, put the veil over my face and play at funerals. Conversations I overheard often turned on my going first to the grave's remaining space. Solemn journeys to the cemetery continued through many years; I would not be drawn away from where my father lay. Not until I left Ireland, when sixteen, did I realize how desolate, how forlorn was the ugliness of those acres of the dead that once seemed so beautiful. Bitterly then, I wrote:

> *It is there on the hillside,*
> *Despicable and disgusting,*
> *Like a white spreading sore*
> *In the flesh;*
> *A contradiction of life*

Spit of the Ould Da

Growing ulcerous in the warmth
Of the town.
'Here is the memory enshrined'
Say the implacable marbles,
Regimented with hard corners
Into rows, and rows, and rows
And rows.

It is there on the hillside,
Fenced in and bordered
By the flaking iron fence
With spear tops to keep
The living out and the dead in.
It is a scurvy patch
Beloved by some but forgotten by most.
'Here lies my husband or son'
Says the expensive masonry
In squat black letters,
A funk alphabet speaking in hard terms
Of cash, and cash, and cash
And cash.

'I will make you this one
For twenty pounds.'
But really the memory
Is still in the house and the heart.
The shadow that fell in the doorway
Across the hallway into the little room
Is blotted out by the passing
And the sun.
The hand that winds up the clock
On the mantelpiece
(Where the photograph once stood)
Is unused to the peculiar

Spit of the Ould Da

Clicking
Of the mechanism, that will
Let the numbered minutes fall out.

One pilgrimage has already been made
And the broken heart gorged on the poison
Of the dead
With horror and pleasure.
Really of course it is nonsense.
Perhaps in a cloud or the wind,
Or in the empty place in the bed,
Or unseen in the crowded street
On Saturday.
Or even, in the mind only,
Or not at all.
But here, under this fester
On the hillside
Could never lie
The faint sweat-smelling flesh
That was loved
Until, and until, and until
And until.

Entry Landscape

✣

Fly, our red-setter bitch, was the champion of the Bog Meadows—even the Mickeys on the farther side of the Blackstaff had to admit that. She flashed through the rushy steppes like a wild-fowler's dream. But when my father died, we lost Fly. And the pigeons went too, for Big 'Ina held superstitions about going into the loft.

All we had was a lecherous tom-cat. His nocturnal forays and wooings invariably brought an assortment of missiles to the backyard wall. By daytime he seldom stirred from the kitchen hearth, where he dozed recuperating and effusing his tom-cat propensities into the atmosphere.

In addition, there were the birds. Dozens of sparrows lined the telegraph wires that ran parallel with the railway like crotchets on staves. Between the backyards and the paling of disused wood sleepers tipped with barbed wire, that fenced off the railway, was a narrow lane called the entry. Belfast was full of entries. Feeding starlings in our entry caused much controversy, and nearly as many squabbles as amongst the starlings themselves. My mother sided with those opposing the leaving of crumbs in the entry, for she had a horror of the rats which came through the paling from the railway banks to share the bread. The menace of our tom-cat did not stay the rats from invading the house.

I badly wanted a dog of my own, a red setter of course,

and preferably one of Fly's handsome progeny that followed the Sunday wild-fowlers. Still, I could always go to the Bog Meadows to catch spricks in the many little streams that fed the Blackstaff. For this, I chose children from the tinkers' tents as companions. The boys of my own street were often too stuck-up because they came from parlour homes.

Among the tinkers lived a number of real Romanies complete with piebalds and caravans of exquisite craftsmanship and colours. A thousand times over would I have preferred one of those shining, rumbling, wander-where-you-will palaces, to the council house with a three-piece bathroom that was my mother's vision. The call of open, rainswept spaces reached out to me, and besides I felt a certain defiance. The more I was told not to go near the tinkers, partly because by repute they liked a slice of child's bottom to fry for breakfast, the more daring I became. Just then, nowhere in the world possessed more allure than the Bog Meadows.

Beautiful hours passed with Mike and Sophie near their tent, or catching frogs and trying to make the spricks go into our nets. Our fishing equipment had to be home-made; poverty left us no alternative. Part of an old silk stocking (more usually lisle) sewn at one end, fastened to a wire ring on the end of a broomstick, provided our way of catching minnows. We sieved through the water, enmeshing the struggling things in the soft stocking. Using hooks was of no use, for the tiny fish were destined for life in a jam-jar on the backyard window-sill.

Did ever child enjoy such delights? We tried to jump across the small streams, and falling in, scrambled quickly out again, careless of clothes, before the black leeches would suck all our blood away, which we relished as a great horror. And if it rained we would lie on the old mattress that so sensibly covered the whole floor of Mike's and Sophie's home, telling impossible tales and listening to the rain falling on a desolated world outside. When the sun shone we would go picking may flowers, piss-a-beds, and snapping lads—the Himalayan balsam predominated in our marshy wilderness—and when hungry we put sour docks between our potato farls.

And when glorious day declined, and the encroaching night stole first the hills and then even the flowers from sight, we crouched near the tent. Passing a grey hand over the landscape as though smoothing a puckered brow, the gloaming engulfed us. Its silence penetrated the laughter of our shinhates, as we sat round the hundred-eyed fire, an Argus which spied brightly on a hundred of our evenings. In lulls between our chatter, the silence washed in like a warm, embracing wave. Then, comfortingly, the thud of the piebald's dung would sound, but loud in the quietness as the roar of the Derry Express.

Coming home at night with my wild flowers, my head full of the well-spent, idyllic hours, I was often jeered at. But God help the boy who called out if alone; I was never 'yella', or scared of anyone my size or under. Many the black eye I gave and encountered, for this or that cause or no cause at all.

Nobody ever called my courage to account. I ran more often than anyone else under the belly of the bread-server's horse, between the heavy-hooved legs, a test of our daring powers. Nevertheless, people regarded me as peculiar because I was a boy and loved flowers, and also hated games like football, cricket and marleys. The round glass marbles, marvellously twisted and spiralled with bright columns of colour, seemed far too beautiful to chip or make dull by spinning them over the pavements.

Other boys roamed the Bog Meadows, in packs, armed with catapults. And this I hated, too, orginating perhaps from a story heard and experience gained at school. Part of our education consisted in giving verbal descriptions of coloured pictures pinned to the blackboard, and this had to be done standing in front of the class. When my turn came I had to give my own account of a sloppy little boy in the background of one print, who was throwing bread to some large birds. Haltingly the words stumbled out, and then I got to the part about him feeding the geese. Swish! on my calf came the cane; swans, I was told, not geese. This was my first public caning; the sting and suddenness of it took me by surprise. Geese, went on the teacher, could be eaten, but not swans. Swans were special birds, always to be treated with great care, and terrible things would happen to the boy who touched one.

And the fairy-tale of Tuan mac Cairill, how it set my mind fluttering with superstitions! This ancient Ulster chieftain, we were told, in addition to living as a man, laid claims to having done so as a stag, a pig, a bird, and a salmon. What a delight to hear of his reincarnation as a hawk, and his cave on the coast from which to fly over all Ireland, knowing every mountain, field, and cottage.

My imagination set to work over the endless possibilities of the soul's transmigration! Up in the cemetery I had noticed a robin fly down many times where I sat. His perky, inquisitive look fascinated me. In my fancy, I imagined the bird always to be the same one, until at last I convinced myself it possessed a human spirit, probably my father's. Killing birds with catapults was murder.

Being prevented by my private reason from a boy's instincts for shooting, I contented myself with tormenting the girls in our street. Making a pea-shooter from a stem of scabby-gub we shot red berries at their legs. Though putting the hemlock to our mouths did not frighten us, the red jack-in-the-box did, terribly. A boy who lived near us ate some, and had to have the back of his throat tickled by a feather until the poison came up.

Entry Landscape

The love of birds engendered by my quaint and temporary faith of transmigration became ingrained. I have never lost it. But for a long time my passions were roused to an intense degree by the sight of birds in trouble. There was the deep and terrible concern I had in the Bog Meadows one night.

Already the years were slipping rapidly by; I was then eight. Leaping from bank to bank of the small shucks, I wanted to get to the far side of the Blackstaff before darkness swallowed up the Meadows. Already the gloaming had settled down, which beset the damp land with such eeriness, and I was on the wrong side, the Mickeys'; I did not much fancy being caught. Then jumping a stream, hurrying, hurrying away from the mountain towards the street lights glimmering at the gloom's edge, I found the wounded whooper-swan.

Poor whooper. It must have food. My dread of the Mickeys evaporated, and realization came that here in the stranded swan, I had found a perfect pet at last. My lanky legs had never carried me so fast. Breathless I arrived home, collected what I could find, and rushed into the darkness again, my heart pounding with the urgency of my errand. Unless I went like the wind, the whooper might die before I reached it. Stumbling over the slippery stepping-stones across the Blackstaff, laden with pieces of soda farls and balm brack, I became vaguely aware that darkness no longer held any terrors for me.

Next day I mitched school and spent wonderful, tender hours with the swan. Then on my next visit, when I returned again to feed it, my whooper had gone. Nothing was left except scattered feathers. The fowlers' dogs must have got it. I took up one of the white feathers, stroked it and carried it carefully home. It became a precious, sad possession of mine for many years after.

The most serious threat to my enjoyment of life came from

school. The Bog Meadows taught me more than ever did the classroom. And the classroom smelt more from sneaks than ever did our kitchen from the tom-cat. The Tit Queen encouraged tale-bearers. If a boy stole the ink with which to do ridiculous homework (and what could be a more logical conclusion than to use *their* ink for *their* work?) a mean classmate usually informed against him. Or in the wretched, drab square of asphalt that formed our playground if a boy scoffed at niceties and did his piddle where he wanted, some toady was sure to blab in the teacher's ear that Willie Burns had done number one over Sammy Brown. And then Tit Queen would bear down, her bosoms like a galleon's sails, waddling towards the culprit saying with poisonous sweetness 'A wee birdie has just told me . . .'

But by this time, fate intervened and saved me from a too-continuous association with school and suchlike. Already I had been into hospital several times, going regularly, in the periods between, to a tuberculosis clinic. Free malt and emulsion never brightened my 'white churchyard dial' as my face was called. My chances of survival were thin and I knew it. Not that morbid feelings set in at the thought of death; rather the contrary, I looked forward to returning to earth as a bird.

My first visitation in this form, planned in solitary moments, I determined should be to the school. What pranks I would play on the Tit Queen, such as dropping spiders down the suggestive gap behind the modesty vest that stretched so obscenely over her breasts; or hopping across the big school register with dirty claws, so that she would have to go on repeated errands to borrow the ink eraser from the headmaster's office. In other fantastic daydreams I wandered into banks and picked up pound notes in my beak to drop down Big 'Ina's chimney.

With that alchemy of a child's mind that can turn anything to gold, I mysteriously linked bird-flight with my father. The boundary of reality dissolved mistily in my dreaming and longing. Even a pair of binoculars that I owned later did not dispel my mystical vision. When old enough to ride on lorries' tailboards out of Belfast into the country, I followed the flappings of whaap and snaw cock with such intentness that often it seemed as if at last I had, nirvana-like, reached my feathered incarnation.

And orthodox religion, far from conflicting with these aerial notions, fostered them. Return to earth in bird form appeared to me as the only tangible thing in the whole business. The parish churches, dull and forbidding, were bare of all iconography—our stiff, unrelenting Protestant beliefs allowed us no figures or pictures. Exceptions were the huge swan-winged angels, which hovered over us with sentimental Protestant faces and nightshirts. And angels were not the only birds we had; in church, to match the pulpit, was an enormous brass eagle cock for a lectern.

Pictures of the Sacred Heart, or of Our Lady, were regarded with horror, but a representation of the Holy Ghost was allowed—in the shape of a dove. Among the crowded acres of the cemetery, where good Protestants lay waiting for the last trump and the final flurry of wings from heaven, a thick choir of the swan-limbed angels kept watch. And hardly a grave that had not a small stone dove crouched in the grass. My father had one.

And since birds sang incessantly, making a stream of their music that babbled invisibly amongst the tombstones, I was utterly sure that all birds were returned souls. At least, so I understood, for a time, as it went without saying that at the Last Judgement the feathers would go and we would all be changed into sheep and goats, so that the Good Shepherd would know the difference between Protestants and Catholics. Small wonder we thought it better to die, than ever let a drop of goat's milk pass our lips.

Entry Landscape

In the early days, before I came by the precious binoculars and was as free as a tinker, a ban was often put on my meandering in the Bog Meadows. No doubt my mother thought the damp bogs bad for me. At other times her reason in keeping me at home was the simple one of guarding the house and the washing.

Although she got up before five during winter months to stoke a boiler, and thereby earn a few extra pennies, in addition to her all-year-round charring, my mother also did piles of washing. Sheets and billowing combinations filled our entry with festoons, the like of which I have only seen in Naples' tall, narrow slum streets that are draped to exclude the impeccable Italian sun.

We children guarded the washing against dirt rather than thieves. Thieves there certainly were, not excluding young men and old ones, tempted irresistibly by the bloomers. A worse danger came from dirty hands, for our entry gave a short cut through from the railway coalyards. The youths and men going home in dungarees made black and shiny from a mixture of sweat and coaldust thought nothing of roughly pushing the curtain of wet washing aside. The black smears meant nothing to them, but hours of work and despair for Big 'Ina. We had to be quick and make a way through the labyrinth before the damage occurred.

Also, the coalbrick men came down that way with asses and carts. Our man was religious, otherwise 'saved'. He handed out gospel tracts with the black bricks of compressed coaldust which we, like many of our neighbours, burnt in lieu of lump coal. His little brother had charge of the ass and, alas, he suffered from the falling sickness. When they trundled down the rough alleyway between the forbidding railway paling and the decaying backyard walls, we always rushed out to stare at him, half in dread, half in hope that he would drop and perform his epileptic antics.

31

Entry Landscape

The *chiaroscuro* of our world was all black and white; kindness and cruelty contrasted sharply; the subtler tones lying between extremes never arose. Those who suffered from a deformity were tormented because of it. Perhaps a limp or a hunched back reminded us too forcibly of our own vulnerability. Bad luck we knew was no respecter of persons. Such things could, and often did, happen to us and ours. Cissy, my sister, wore glasses and was taunted with 'Speccy-four-eyes'. She contented herself with the stock reply:

> *Sticks and stones may break my bones,*
> *But names will never hurt me,*
> *And when I'm dead and in my grave*
> *You'll suffer what you called me.*

Being a boy, when others shouted after me because of my thin, pallid face, I could reply more effectively by fists. But I, too, played a part in baiting the unfortunate. At one time we hounded the mute. He stood for hours every day on the railway bridge, terrifying, half human, half monster. Out of the steam clouds surging up from a train passing underneath, his form emerged, slumped against the parapet. The steam was supernatural, the mute oozed horror. We hated him, and keeping a safe distance, hurled abuse at him, hoping he would chase us, though knowing that with his deformed legs he would never catch us.

Fortunately, and equally thoughtlessly, we reserved for blind people a special kindness. A home for the blind existed near our street and perhaps because their disability did not parade itself in grotesque forms, we accepted them. We even protected them. A gang of boys, to which I later belonged, beat up a boy who had stolen from the blind pedlar who sold pathetic wares at the football ground. To teach the boy a lesson, and to use his crime as an excuse for cruelty of our own, we forced him to perform outrageous rituals.

Entry Landscape

The log-sawing sound of the coal donkey braying in the entry was a sign to my mother of approaching rain and meant that the washing must be taken in. I never thought to verify her belief; it rained so frequently and the donkey brayed so often that the two could hardly help coinciding. Even the coalbrick man must have considered his ass a notorious brayer, for it was said that on Armistice Day he tied up the animal's jaw for fear it should break the two minutes of silence.

In school we had our own distraction on November 11th. The teachers lined us up in the playground and a Boys' Brigade bugler strutted and blew his blasts into the echoing landscape of bricks and slates around us. A girl in my class fainted during the silence. Ever after she was regarded with some awe, as though the stigmata had exhibited themselves.

When winter took itself off and we no longer needed coalbricks to keep out the gnawing cold, Big 'Ina washed our blankets, too. Gone were the dark nights when my little sister Helen was too scared to cross the backyard to the lavatory. Instead, across the Bog Meadows from the hills of beyond, spring airs blew, and the sun lingered wanly a few minutes longer every day, its beams unnoticed among the grinding city's chimney. The men pressing home in the evening down the entry could see their way then. Heaven help them should they smear black hands over the dripping blankets, especially if Granny Harbinson's patchwork quilt that took two years to make, should be hanging out.

Sweet spring was the season when we opened our shops in the entry. Along the row of identical backyard doors the counters would be set up in the openings. Behind these cardboard boxes and packing cases that had escaped a fate as winter firewood, groups of children set out their wares. We arranged piles of broken glass and fragments of coloured china, old toffee papers were screwed round stones, and chips

C   33

of wood disguised in chocolate wrappings. God knows, our make-belief shops held more promise for us than real ones.

On Friday mornings when dustbins stood out for emptying, we rummaged through them to find stock for our shops. But imitating reality, our plenitude could only be got for money, though this was easier to come by than the real thing, for we used pieces of china with gold edges. Friends of the great-aunts once asked us to stay at their house. But it was not the number and size of their rooms, compared with our own small house, that staggered me, but real wealth represented by a fabulous collection of blue, gold-rimmed plates. Half a dozen received immediate attention by the hammer I brought from a kitchen drawer. I hid the pieces away for use as shop money when we got home. The friends never, of course, invited us again.

For a change from shops we played hospitals. As in our family, most of the children knew the inside of one fairly intimately. Old tarpaulins that normally covered mangles standing in the backyards, were set up as tents in the entry. Popular consent often chose me as doctor, while the bold hussies stripped off and contorted themselves or made groans and wry faces, meant to be symptomatic of the most outrageous and impossible illnesses.

And then winter quite forgotten, yet long before the purple charlies and bluebells lured us to the woods and fields fringing the city, we started our May Queens. Nothing could have induced us to wait until April was out. Up and down both sides of the street went groups in support of their queen. Being unusually beautiful, our Helen was always chosen. I had to be the Darkie. What a performance I went through, scraping the chimney for soot to blacken myself. Gorgeously apparelled, 'got up', we said, the Queen paraded in clothes of vivid crêpe paper. She and the Darkie danced and capered, at the same time resting one hand on a pole carried by two attendants. These lackeys also carried empty cocoa tins for collecting halfpennies and farthings. As we danced we chanted tunelessly, special May Queen rhymes,

> *Our Queen up the river*
> *With a ya . . . ya . . . ya . . .*
> *Our Queen is G.O.O.D.*
> *G.O.O.D., G.O.O.D. . . .*

And when it came to the line, 'Our nig can burl the pole, burl the pole,' I, as nigger, had to spin over and under the pole. Our amusement did not always remain so innocent; battle was given when rival queens met, particularly if money had been obtained from a house deaf to the entreaties of previous callers. Hair came out in handfuls, the paper clothes became tattered shreds, all queenly etiquette forgotten.

Whatever funds accrued from the May Queens, quickly dissolved again. We turned satisfied steps first of all to the ice-cream parlour where, despite a firm belief that the old hag mixed it in the po, we thought the best ices our side of Sandy Row could be got.

After the sweet ices, the next course of our feast was a warm-up at the grocer's with a halfpennyworth of hot peas and vinegar, served in a cup complete with spoon. Sweets did not come very high in our list of delicacies, and often as not we bought a pennyworth of tripe from the butcher, and ate it raw. My mother did this, too, calling in with her penny as she came late from work. Our favourite thing to chew, and in fact all over Ulster, was dulse, a dried seaweed sold in the greengrocer's. Younger children chewed farthing sticks of cinnamon bark perhaps because its taste was not so sharp and salty as dulse, and they also tried their hand at smoking it like cheroots.

I never ventured in the greengrocer's nearest home, for the woman who owned it regarded me as dangerous and kept a sharp look-out. With my friends I would stand outside the shop and pretend to look in the windows while our fingers picked busily at the fruit and vegetables in boxes on the pavement. Once, the woman pursued me down the street, into our house and to the very glory-hole under the stairs, brandishing a cabbage whose heart I had completely eaten.

Scavenging, too, could be profitable, when funds such as came from May Queens were not to be had. One of the best places was a sweetshop run by an old dame. For the affluent, halfpenny pokes provided a thrill. She filled newspaper cones with a selection of sweets and broken biscuits, and set them out on a tray, from which a choice could be made. One of the pokes was 'lucky' for inside a halfpenny would be hidden.

Besides this special attraction, the sweet-woman made honeycombs and sometimes threw them away because they had burnt or would not rise, and then the most delectable sticky pieces could be taken from her dustbin. We could be certain to find left-overs at the back of a chain store's local branch. There in wooden barrels, overlooked by a careless salesgirl, juicy grapes could be won by sieving through the sawdust packing. And if fruit dominated our mood, then outside the big bakery piles of apple peelings waited to be plundered.

On rare occasions the shops offered their goods free over the counter, so that backyard hunting was unnecessary. But then, of course, there were limiting conditions. A men's outfitters in our part of the town, once had the idea of holding a Cap Week. Nothing but caps crammed their window, except a small space left clear at the front, and in this temporary pen, some tortoises crept miserably round and round. Some had letters painted on their shells. If you could entice them to line up in order, so that they spelled out c-a-p-s, and were first into the shop, then you got a free cap. What weary hours I spent at that window trying to coax the slow creatures into position by tapping on the window. The possible tortoise permutations were too great, I never got my cap.

Not far from the tortoises, Aggie Moore kept a second-hand clothes shop. Probably without being too much off the mark, people affectionately called it 'Aggie Moore's Flea Circus'. Aggie herself, frail and aged, presided from the back where she ensconced herself with a witch's ball and a good sup of red biddy. I thought her fascinating despite an element of fear induced by her crystal gazings.

Aggie was kind, and people presumed upon her in consequence. When a neighbour of ours was fined for neglecting his greyhound, Aggie bought the dog after the law case was over. But poor Sal, the dog, was a bone of contention for years. Aggie loved the animal so much that she regularly paid out sums demanded in blackmail by the former owner's wife who claimed Sal as hers.

I loved the dog, a mousey, pointed, nervous animal, and when I was older, Aggie trusted me to take it out to the Bog Meadows for exercise. But I had always strict instructions never to let Sal off the lead, and if suspicious characters approached her, always to race home to the Flea Circus, for Aggie was obsessed that her beloved would be kidnapped. One day when I called to take Sal out, I found the shop locked up, and the dog in a frenzy inside. She tore through a huge tick, smothering the whole shop with a layer of snowy feathers.

Aggie's fame rested in her ability as a seer, and I long determined that when I got my first pay-packet at fourteen, part of it would go to Aggie who should do me a reading at the ball. Because I was such a good friend to Sal, she had given me a quick summing-up of my hands, but the ball, of course, could only be done when I was a proper workman. That she was proficient in her black art, received ample testimony from her prophecy that Prince Eddy would never wear the crown. Nearer home one of my mother's best friends had a reading. 'Very soon', warned Aggie in the seance, 'you'll lose a loved one,' and the woman went home to find that during the absence, her husband had deserted her to run across the water. After that nobody doubted that Aggie Moore was indeed a witch, though we liked her none the less for that.

Resort to Aggie Moore's, for either clothes or forecasts, was never made by my mother. Nobody could say that silks and satins ever put out our kitchen fire, for though she delighted in good clothes and longed to be well turned-out, she spent hardly anything on her own back. She certainly possessed no big dresses, except when someone died and relatives presented the clothes. From this source we got *the* fur coat, and rightly indeed wasn't this the talk of the town! Not that my mother ever wore it. The coat remained our principal piece of bedding in the house for years, until we grew up and a proper eiderdown was bought, allowing the grand coat to be converted into a hearthrug for the parlour.

My mother allowed herself no indulgence other than her Sunday diamond. Before going off to Sunday School, I went for the diamond, which cost a penny. The piece of jam sponge covered with white icing, cut into a diamond shape, and eaten with a cup of tea, was her Sunday afternoon treat. But my idea of high living, though it included the Sunday diamond with its succulent icing, ranged further. The Tit Queen's rubber goloshes I thought extremely grand; they expressed a way of life and hinted at luxury undreamed of in our world, where, if it rained, we simply got our plimsolls wet. And my conception of ultimate grandeur was symbolized by the voluminous and dignified curtains in the church, voluptuously red and patterned with fleur-de-lis.

Because of the curtains my fancy ran entirely away with itself, and my love of the theatre was born. I could see myself lording it in the streets, wrapped in a sweeping cloak of the

Entry Landscape

red material. And when the war came, the dream was realized, or almost so. The church had to be equipped with black-out curtains, so down came the old ones, and the congregation set about making the black hangings. Me they employed to thread the needles.

Arriving one night for this bit of war-effort, I found the church empty. This was my chance—I seized a length of the fleur-de-lis cloth, and draping its rich folds about me began a solemn parade down the aisle. I enjoyed its important weight on my shoulders, and the luxurious swish it made behind me over the tiled floor. What a shock I got, when a black-out curtain maker caught me, and asked rudely if I thought myself King Billy? Still, I found some consolation in the thought that at least I must have looked the part.

Pin-Holing

❦

For three months of the year our life, my sisters' and mine, was dominated by the pin-holes. Of its charity the church contributed towards the upkeep of parish orphans, for such we were, five shillings apiece. We therefore were expected to respond by proceeding from house to house, collecting money —after all there was nothing better than a pinched orphan face at the front door to wring hearts and pockets.

Lest the devil should tempt us to misuse the collected cash, the church provided a little blue card, marked off into squares and for every donation of a penny, the card must be pierced with a pin. A simple system, whereby the orphans' honesty could be closely watched, for the number of pennies handed over must equal the number of pin-holes. More bounteous gifts, such as a sixpence or more rarely, a whole shilling, earned the donor a special honour, for their name was inscribed on the reverse side of the card and later printed in the parish magazine.

The collecting became an adventure; it took me to many strange parts of the city and brought me contacts with a multitude of people, all different. It also made an actor of me. It taught me much about human nature, how occasionally men and women can rise to heroism or tragedy, but otherwise normally exist in a banal, petty life. A child of nine or ten making his way out to the Belfast golf-course and walking across the soft turf towards a man-about-town, loud of voice and dress alike; and then presenting the little blue card and asking for a penny so that one more hole could be pierced; and for the said man, well-fed and healthy in addition to being loud, to lie deliberately that he had "no change"—such experiences soon showed me the divisions of men's thinking and giving. Alternatively, I discovered that if a road-sweeper could be waylaid with his Friday pay-packet still in a virgin state, a wing and a pin-hole were almost a certainty.

My two sisters and I, like conquerors, divided the city between us, and my territory often included the farther side of the railway where the rich suburbs lay. Here the toffs lived, together with the government officials, the professors and doctors, and the grand dean with the withered arm. Each house was a new venture, each opening of the door was the curtain going up on a new drama. I never knew what would be revealed. Perhaps I always expected something wonderful to happen, the event that would change our life, and mean that my mother would not have to stay out working so long.

Normally I found nothing more than perhaps a new smell, for the houses could be identified by a smell peculiar to each. At one the odour wafting out as a prim maid answered the bell, might be compounded of various brands of floor polish and disinfectant; another might be more redolent of the dogs that flew out at my legs; a third house might leak smells of delicious cooking, with flavours of dishes whose very existence was unknown to me; and some houses, though strangely not many, smelt powerfully of human beings, and the heady, luxurious perfumes of women with outrageous accents.

The rich in their houses usually remained invisible and delegated the task of dealing with trade to their servants. But I knew them well enough in the streets and how, not once or twice a day, perhaps twice within five minutes, they would angrily wave away the grubby little pin-hole card, and announce with disgust that they had 'no change'. Having made their fortunes from the likes of us and from the mills and factories that scarcely left room for our mean streets to run between, they wanted no other contact with us. It seemed to me that they determined, every fat man jack of them, that not a single penny would they let fall from their tight fists.

In their suburban villas they were even more remote. Standing on the top step I would ask for a penny with the meekness that I had learnt, as a trick of the trade, well became a parish orphan. The worst reception that this request could then receive was to be brutally asked, had I not read the notice on the gate? Far, far worse than the enamel or bronze labels on the gate ferociously warning 'Beware of the Dog' were those which coldly intimated that 'No Hawkers: No Circulars' would be welcomed.

Dogs, even the most savage, could be braved, and sometimes perhaps befriended, and not infrequently the notice was a fraud, for not a growl or a fang would be seen as I advanced up the drive, though this may have been because the canine menace had died, but the bronze notice had been left.

'No Hawkers' signs never lied. At such houses the uniformed maids would take the card off to their mistresses, and in a few moments bring it back with one of the familiar tales, 'Sorry, but we belong to Saint So-and-so's parish,' or, 'Sorry, but we are Methodists, you know,' as though, dear God above, that cleared the world of widows and the fatherless. They were aware, as well as I was, that at their grand church there were no parish orphans to support. Gloomy episodes like these would sometimes be suddenly illuminated by the maid's own kind heart. Hating to turn me away, she would produce a penny of her own.

It might be thought that our enthusiasm in collecting

would be a little dampened by all the refusals and excuses. But we were toughened by experience. 'No change,' 'Sorry, we're Methodists,' 'No Hawkers,' 'My husband sees to all that, and be sure you close the gate,' 'We've had two lots of beggars already today, so I'm afraid I can't,' 'You should be at school, boy, now get along and don't let me see you again'—none of these blunted our persistence.

And this perseverance was not because of our anxiety to fill the church poor-box and so ensure our own income from it, but from an ulterior motive. Our sole object lay in getting one penny more than a target set by the pin-hole organizing secretary. This earned us an invitation to the great anuual bun-fight in the parish hall, a vastly important date in our social calendar. From one year to the next we boasted of how many Devon splits and chocolate eclairs we had gorged—the proud dispatcher of twenty-two cakes having obviously enjoyed the affair more than the better-behaved little girl who managed only four apple tartlets and six coconut snowballs.

For my sisters and me proficiency in pin-hole collecting became part of life and as our skill grew, we waxed more audacious. We never fell short of the target and never missed the banquet. Keeping our little bundles of pennies safely stowed away, so that we could not steal from each other before they were due to be handed in, was the most difficult part of all. Hiding-places had to be found in the roof gutter, under the floorboards, or beneath a favourite sally-bush along the railway verges.

Cissy held the record for collecting in our trio. When not out pin-holing she would be canvassing tickets for church concerts or socials. Her ability amazed even me, hardened as I was to the ways and means of salesmanship. The Girls' Friendly Society recognized her services one year, when she had sold a phenomenal number of tickets for a display, by giving her a magnificent Easter egg. How she prized the oversized chocolate ovoid and its ornate, Baroque flowers and lettering in icing sugar.

The egg must have symbolized some luxury or richness in her mind, for she bore it gingerly home and after proudly displaying it, wrapped the egg again in its box. Definitely, the Easter egg was not to be eaten. But where could so large an object be hidden? None of the usual places would do. An answer was found and the egg disappeared. The next-door neighbour, I was told, had taken it in.

One morning I nested in our outside lavatory, the door, as usual, wide open, for though it possessed no bolt, we liked a view to induce relaxation. And then I noticed a peculiar bulge under the tarpaulin covering our mangle. Yes, it was Cissy's marvellous prize Easter egg. Of course, I only intended to eat one or two of the decorative flowers. But I began then on the shell itself and before I knew it, the beautiful egg had been broken into ruins, and was almost devoured. Cissy tried to murder me when her loss was discovered. I maintained in justification that she was babyish to have thought of such a hiding-place—not that she could have put the egg up the parlour chimney, her usual resort in an emergency.

Compared with the means of keeping our haul of pin-hole pennies the means of getting it were easy. Technique had to be varied to suit the victim. A good method was to stand outside the pubs with a hungry orphan look fixed on your face and present the blue card to anyone who looked sufficiently far gone.

Drunks, we knew, lost their sense of proportion, and if close-fisted when sober, might give surprising amounts when under the influence. Some of them needed to be shepherded home, and often I, along with other boys waiting about specially for this, would lead them away like eighteenth-century link-boys. For this service, too, the rewards were often handsome.

Pin-Holing

Another fruitful method was to gate-crash weddings or funeral parties, wearing the pleading look, for people hated to be thought mean by their neighbours or in-laws. And against courting couples the greatest subtlety could be employed—'Miss, do you think your boy-friend could spare a penny for the orphans?' What would-be husband and father could refuse the pathos of my little one-act play?

I could never really accept the hardness of the human heart. It seemed only natural to me that people would want to give. Whenever they refused, the shock and hurt was new each time. I did not know then, as now I do, about inverse proportion, and that the more money people have the less they are likely to part with.

Innocent and in hope I set out one day, expecting at least a tanner. I had a message to take to the headmistress of the large school where my mother worked as caretaker. My blue card was to go with me and a good appearance was to be made by wearing my best Sunday suit of navy-blue serge. Tricked out, message in pocket, I set off sure of at least a few pin-holes.

I found the woman sitting in her garden, under a shady apple tree, finishing her afternoon tea. A chow, lying at her feet like a lion, stood up and growled when I approached. His mistress, ignoring me for the moment, enticed him away with a slice of ginger cake. My mouth watered, as the dog's black tongue licked the succulent cake. Pacified, the chow reclined again, lowering his head on to his paws, but keeping surly eyes on my every move.

The message part done, I presented the card and began to explain it. But she did not listen, except to the fatal word 'penny'. 'Has your mother sent you here to beg?' she inquired. My blood was up at once, here was the Tit Queen all over again. Scorn and derision. Idle woman sprawled in a basket chair, throwing lumps of ginger cake to an overfed dog, I wanted to take her by the shoulders and shake her. She had not finished. As I left, she remarked that my stockings needed mending.

They were indeed full of holes. But how dare she criticize my mother for not darning them. How dare this fat slug imply that my mother was a good-for-nothing slut. Big 'Ina was already up before five o'clock of a winter morning, with a long walk in front of her, snow, rain and everything, to this woman's own school. It was Big 'Ina who raked, and cleared, and refuelled the boiler that kept the headmistress warm. And this done, she swept and dusted in the numerous classrooms before school began, and then had to walk back to the city again in order to clean our own house, get through the piles of washing, go out shopping, and have a dinner ready for us, when we came in at midday.

This woman with her afternoon tea and unfriendly dog did not realize that Big 'Ina's afternoons were spent doing a char's work down town, scrubbing and brushing, before walking out to the school again, to sweep every classroom once more, to be followed by clearing the playground. Getting home again at seven in the evening, after slaving from five in the morning, was it likely my mother would always feel like darning stockings?

The school boiler haunted Big 'Ina. She lived in terror of its going out, and sometimes after getting our tea, would trail away out once more for a last look at it. If the boiler went out, Big 'Ina thought she would lose the job, and the money that went with it. The long school holidays left her no respite, for then she went to wash and scrub every inch of the great building, besides charring in the town.

The income of a working-class, Belfast family in the late 'thirties averaged between £3 and £5. But the total of all my mother's efforts amounted to no more than £1 4s. 0d. With the orphan fund we received just under £2 all told. Rent took ten shillings. Four people had to live on the remainder. We were indeed in low waters.

I was twelve then, and beginning to learn about inequality. Often enough we sang in church 'All things bright and beautiful', but nearer the truth were the same hymn's 'The rich man in his castle, the poor man at his gate.'

But Big 'Ina never gave in. To clothe us she started a shilling-a-week club for a department store amongst the neighbours. For every £10 worth she sold, the store gave her clothes to the value of £1. In this way we had our suits and dresses, which were always smart and admired by people who wondered how she managed.

Being children we could not know the meaning of Big 'Ina's fight to keep going, nor understand entirely that it was solely on our account. She was only thirty and good-looking, and everyone expected her to marry again. But Big 'Ina knew. She knew what children can suffer—already her relations had pointed out the fact that being 'well connected' she could make good, and as for the children of her previous, mistaken marriage, they could be dumped in an orphanage. Nothing could persuade her to be parted from us. Big 'Ina turned many offers of marriage away, and sacrificed her own life to keep a home going for us.

And often we were her worst enemies. Our hardened, cruel carelessness, the 'back-cheek' and tempers, would only be checked by the sound of the ambulance outside the door, and the sight of Big 'Ina being carried off to hospital. We stole from her and wrecked the home she tried to keep for us. To our shame, one Saturday Cissy and I collected seven shillings of the club money, and spent it on an excursion to the sea at Bangor. There, my sister was soon whisked away by a British soldier although she was only thirteen years old. I was left with a bottle of lemonade and a heavy feeling inside. It was my first taste of real remorse.

Pin-Holing

Every halfpenny in our house had to be carefully accounted for, every pile of cinders carefully sifted. And Big 'Ina's only rewards—the Sunday diamond, our rebellious love, and perhaps a discarded dress from one of the religious cousins. What number of mornings did I not hear her wandering in the pre-dawn blackness, waiting for the engine-drivers to go by to the railway yards, so that she could ask for a match to make her breakfast of tea? What deaths of shame and pride did she not suffer to borrow a gill of milk, a neighbour's hat to go to church, or the skin of an egg-shell to put over my blistered heels?

I was not always unconscious of the struggle, especially in that awful, terrifying silence of the night when I tossed in bed, sleepless with worry, thinking I would never hear her weary footsteps coming down the street, and her hollow cough on the stairs.

But she always came.

'Keep us and the childer', she mumbled at the side of the bed, gave herself a good scratch, and tried to get a share of the bed without waking my sisters.

Something of Big 'Ina's stamina must have passed on to me, for even after my reception in the headmistress's garden, I did not give up pin-holing. Instead I put out my tongue when out of sight and scrawled obscene words in the sheen of dust on her car. As good fish in the sea as ever came out, there were other houses, other stages for my little play.

I discovered the weather had considerable influence on collecting. Rainy days seemed to soften people's hearts. It was certainly the rain that led me inside the Chinese collector's house, and so, through the years, into his affection and regard. Here was the obverse of our life's penny, a triumph over the 'No change.'

The strange old man had his house on the road next to the headmistress. It was filled with fabulous Chinese porcelain. Perfume sprinklers, pilgrim bottles, lotus bowls, and perforated boxes to hold fighting crickets in captivity, were crammed on shelf and overmantel; while round the walls stood enormous trumpet-mouthed vases bigger than myself. The dogs of Fu, with bared fangs and curling tongues in green and gold, growled from amongst diminutive landscapes and pastoral scenes of yellow fields red with flowers. The statuette of an emperor had real hair and the same laughing dial of wrinkles as the owner. A cage of Pekin robins, reaching from floor to ceiling, occupied one corner of his living-room.

On the first call at the house, I really looked the part of a destitute orphan. Fortunately it had been raining for hours, my plimsolls squelched and left pools of water at every step like a badly house-trained puppy, while my jersey clung and stretched in a sodden, shapeless mess.

The old man looked in astonishment at the dripping thing that stood on his doorstep. Peering over half-moon glasses, he flapped about me like a hen, conducted me into the living-room, and sat me on a high uncomfortable chair before a fire that leapt and crackled up the chimney. A basin of hot water was brought and he proceeded to wash my feet, solemnly, like an abbot before a monk in the *Mandatum* ablutions of Holy Week.

Finding myself in no danger, I let my eyes wander, over the Chinese porcelain and the rod-puppets, from the old man himself to the corner aviary. The tiny birds which hopped and twittered with fastidious delicacy, fascinated me. What a fabulous addition to the list of names in my naturalist's notebook they would make. I asked the strange man for their name and wanted him to write it down. Astonishment changed to enthusiasm and he begged me to let him see the jottings. When my plimsolls and feet dried and were warmed through at the fire I thought it time to move on. At the door my benefactor placed both hands on my head, abstracted his gaze dramatically towards heaven and called down a blessing.

Pin-Holing

I thought he was 'barmy'. But all the same I went next day to show my notes on bird-watching, and frequently afterwards, knowing I would come away having pockets lined with the price of several cinema seats, and lots of pin-holes into the bargain.

The old collector and his exotic environment grew on me. He became Uncle Hughie, and in later years the house became my home. I knew him for scarcely more than a year before the war carried me away from Belfast. His strongest influence in my life began when I was fourteen and had come back from the country to begin work in the shipyard.

But in the earliest days of our relationship, he played the important half, always pressing gifts on me. I treasured those oriental oddments, imagining them to be of tremendous value. He presented me with two huge coloured photographs taken during his travels in the East.

The 'Great Gate of Nikko' with its fearsome dragon masks and hanging bells, and the deep, twisted roof thick with carving underneath, wakened a strong desire in me. I wanted to go and see these things in reality. When I thought that the strange and beautiful land could be reached by simply boarding a boat in Belfast harbour, steaming round the world, and stepping off at the other end, it seemed I could not grow up quickly enough.

Was it possible I would ever walk over the curious matting of a Japanese house, and see with my own eyes the crouching figures of Uncle Hughie's 'Ceremony of Samurai' photograph? Would I ever see the partly shaved heads that made the performers look like badgers, and hear the rustle of their wonderfully embroidered, padded dresses?

So in this way I discovered early my obsession for travelling, though it had to wait years for fulfilment. And my pleasure in the weird architecture had to spend itself in more mundane affairs. Though possessing no clear idea of what architecture really was, the thought often occurred that our little house would be improved out of recognition if the wall between parlour and kitchen were knocked down.

Though marvellous possessions the coloured photographs were to me; and luxurious the dates and sweets that smacked distinctly of camphor balls; and fabulous almost beyond believing the Javanese shadow-puppets that danced on the old man's walls; and practically unprecedented the whole Christmas shilling Uncle Hughie gave—of all these, none could compare with the binoculars.

A rush of conflicting emotions fought for expression as he handed them to me, as he gave me the key, not to a new world, but one I had known and inhabited since my first visits to the Bog Meadows. It was the world of the sky and the water reeds where my silent friends wheeled on strong pinions or rode the little waves chopped by the wind into the lake.

Now I could follow them as if their wings were mine, and when they swooped down, rushing like meteors, or when they up-breasted to the highest pinnacles of cloud, I could go with them. If necessary I would lay down my life in defence of the binoculars, and sell my stout Protestant soul before I would part with the crystal lenses. I knew all this as I took his gift, but could not say it. He must have understood, for he made the binoculars mine because I had so admired the Pekin robins that fluttered among the pilgrim bottles and lotus bowls.

Chorus Boy

Scarlet, scarlet, though your sins be scarlet,
They shall be white as snow in the precious blood.

So ran the rollicking chorus we sang in many a mission hall. To impress the awful colour fully on the minds of his infant audience, one evangelist I heard stood on the platform with a glass of raspberryade in one hand and a glass of milk in the other. Not only did the liquids symbolize respectively sin and purity, but at the end of his talk he dispensed the milk. Naturally, I had not behaved well enough to merit this reward. In any case, the raspberryade would have appealed to me more, though I cannot remember whether this was given away too. Perhaps, because of its evil associations, it was poured down the sink.

Scarlet was undoubtedly the colour of sin, for in addition to the Scarlet Woman of Rome who ruled the Mickeys, there was also the red rope. Inspired by the harlot of Jericho, we regarded a red rope hanging from upper-storey windows as the sign of a brothel. But try as I would, I could never find one in our city, though I imagined the streets of London and Liverpool to be festooned with crimson cords.

The colour symbol, far from clarifying the subject of sin, only confused it. I sang as lustily as the next about scarlet sins, but remained baffled. And this was because of the Salvation Army people, who, although I knew them to be godly, wore splendid scarlet jerseys. One of my plump cousins had the Army bonnet, and my mother often declared that she was a 'good livin' wee girl'. But why did she dress like the Woman of Rome?

In our district the Salvation Army held considerable sway. Sunday morning calm, that blessed the streets after a rowdy Saturday night, would be solemnized by the blissful sounds of the Army band. It sounded like angel music. And the rattle of tambourines, like reeds shaken by the wind, brought many a man to his front door. A glimpse of a rosy-cheeked girl, squeezed into a uniform, beating her hands on the tambourine's stretched skin, made manly hearts thump with the same rhythm.

We thought Salvationists odd, and not only because they clad themselves in the sin colour. They would never cook on Sundays, but ate corned-beef instead, so that the womenfolk could go off to attend Holiness at the citadel. We sang a jingle,

> *The Salvation Army is free from sin,*
> *They all go to heaven in the corned-beef tin,*
> *The corned-beef tin is made of glass*
> *So they all fall down and break their ass.*

The Army waged a never-ending war against drink. Bottle-fights meant something different to them—the bottle being their enemy. We had a rare time on Saturday nights when converted drunks gave public testimonies of redeeming power. They wallowed in a morass of former sins, sometimes in most entertaining and gruesome detail. The fallen were exhorted to follow them to the penitents' stool.

One such circle of Salvationists gathered every Saturday almost opposite Moses Hunter's pub down town in the big square. While I kept a weather-eye open for a drunk to link-arm home, the evangelist would be scattering invitations to the 'real home in glory'. Drink and the devil were one and the same to the Army. And once a man was born again he must,

> *Dare to be a Daniel,*
> *Dare to stand alone,*
> *Ne'er to stand in a public house,*
> *Bring your money home.*

My own religion, like Sam's in *Poor Richard's Almanack*, was very much of a Cheddar cheese, made from the milk of one-and-twenty parishes. Dozens of churches and mission halls clotted the streets of our neighbourhood, and up near the cemetery stood the Mickeys' 'chapels'. Notice-boards and wayside pulpits displaying warnings of the 'wrath to come' seemed to be more numerous than the sign of the three brass balls. Many more church doors swung open than ever jug-and-bottle entrances.

But what could be found inside when the doors were opened? Division. All Ireland was divided, the border cut the north from the south, and Mickeys from Protestants, and at the Last Day, the goats would be divided from the sheep. And so even with the mission halls, they took their stand either behind belief in the Second Blessing on the one hand, or disbelief in it on the other. Theological nuances subtler than this passed over their heads. Personally, I was out for any sort of blessing, no matter what the source, so long as it kept me from early bed. 'Showers of blessing we need', was my motto like the hymn-writer. Second or otherwise, I took my blessings where they could be found—I went everywhere.

Invincible though the Salvation Army was, even mightier, especially in numbers, were the Plymouth Brethren. Division cankered the Brethren too, for one sect was Open, and the other Closed. Banners flying and sandwich-boards donned like armour, our local Open conducted street services. High-blood-pressure-faced brothers droned at the dreary tunes of Moody and Sankey. Others shouted themselves righteously hoarse with alternate promises of golden gates, crystal seas, and the city of twelve foundations where no night was, and threats of lakes of fire and everlasting torment.

One crumpled old Brother, fighting a lone campaign, crept along like a beetle carrying his sandwich-board. On the front, in bold capitals, was 'I AM A FOOL', with 'For Christ's sake' in smaller type. People turned to laugh as he went by, and read on the back, 'But whose fool are you?'. The particular spiritual wilderness in which he chose to cry was that of the football ground, where among the crowds wasting time and eternity at the match, he wandered up and down looking forlorn, silently witnessing.

But doctrine did not concern us and we youngsters liked the Plymouth Brethren, because on Monday evenings a rousing children's service was held in their hall. Hundreds went, where we could yell in chorus as hard as lungs would go, 'I am H-A-P-P-Y' and 'I am S-A-V-E-D'.

At one end of the hall a huge roll was suspended from the ceiling. The great pages bore the chorus words, and the conductor pointed to each one, because we were very young, and our proficiency at reading was of a very minor order. He also turned the huge leaves over with his stick.

Pedalling away furiously at the harmonium, as though going up-hill on a bicycle, sat the Driver. A little, round woman with an enormous bun of white hair, she was inexhaustibly patient and kind-hearted. But we did not name her the Driver because of the way she rode the harmonium. We teased her unmercifully. Seldom could she perch on the organ stool without some instrument aimed at her, a catapult, spittle-sodden paper, or a pen-nib dart.

A record could not be kept numbering the occasions when the Driver threw herself on to the stool, painfully to realize it had been loaded with tin-tacks or drawing-pins. On finding toffee-papers stuck round her hat, she would hold them in

front of her like an offering, close her eyes, and pray audibly
'Drive them out Lord! Drive them out!' We did not know
she was exorcizing the evil spirits in us, but simply thought
she wanted us cleared out of the hall. And so she became the
'Driver'.

After the service we made a rush to certain wealthy Brethren who distributed coppers to our wild cries of 'Penny
Mister!'

'Have you met the Lord yet?' the Brother would enquire of
a less-forward little girl. And we would drown her answer
with our lies—'I have Mister. Honest! Och go on, give us a
penny!'

Lucky ones would force open the Brethren's hands, sometimes to meet with disappointment and find only a gilt medal
there inscribed 'God is love'. We had so many little medals,
but coppers were always scarce.

Near a bridge spanning the railway, stood an iron hut, the
Wee Mission. For a wager of half-a-slab of chocolate-covered
toffee I put up my hand to be 'saved' at one of their meetings.
I was ten years old. This outward sign, of which the inward
grace was entirely lacking, pleased the preacher and congregation, who gave it as good a reception as they knew how by
singing,

> *Tell my mother what her boy has done*
> *God has spoken to her wayward son;*
> *To be honest till the crown is won:*
> *Oh Lord, I'm coming home.*

It was no mean feat I had performed, for my younger sister
and her friends were present. They turned to stare at me,
pointing sceptical fingers. Our 'saved' neighbours who were
there, and who like the Army's ex-drunks could give excellent
testimonies of former sinful lives, complete with penitential
tears, were amazed. They felt genuinely sorry for my mother.

Chorus Boy

In their view my father had been a 'waster', and I, her only son, had already been in 'trouble' several times.

Outside, after the histrionics were over, I got the toffee prize from my friend, and ran off behind the bakery, where one wall was always warm, and the air sweet with the aroma of fresh baking. For weeks after I fled out of the back, whenever I heard the front-door knocker. Someone whispered that the Elders of the Wee Mission knew that my performance in the hall had only been foxing about. Severe punishment would descend on mockers, I thought, though to give the Elders their due, I came to no harm.

Like connoisseurs we picked and chose carefully from the extensive menu of choice religious dishes. A firm favourite were the meetings of sects believing in baptism by immersion. Here we could have our fill of comedy and thrills, spiced with the possibility of an accident. Steam rising from the big tank that represented the Jordan, filled us with passions like those of ancient Romans in the Colosseum, the baptismal waters were our arena.

Our gladiator might be a bold huzzy, no longer robed in sin-scarlet but in a long white nightdress, ready to go down under. Or another might be some elderly soul, born again only very late in life. Here the thrill intensified. We wanted blood. With any luck the frail body, clad in white, would struggle at the last minute against the head being pushed under the water. Would the old worn-out heart stand up to the shock, and the emotional strain of being made whole preparatory to entering the full fellowship of the breaking of bread? Breathless we waited, hoping against hope for a fainting fit or a wrestling sinner.

A café in the city, fashionable at that time, attracted its customers by making snacks in the shop-window. And inside pretty but supercilious waitresses in saucy uniforms served the smart society who frequented the place. One of these waiting

57

goddesses, known popularly as Hot Ruby, found salvation with a totally-immersing sect. In due course the buxom, come-hither wench, now vulgarly called Bible Ruby, was led to the waters. All eyes in the hall followed the voluptuous figure shrouded in the baptismal nightdress, as it went to receive a blessing in the tank. The little man, who was standing in for John the Baptist, supported her as she leaned backwards. Then her great weight seemed to be too much for him. Bible Ruby grabbed at him, and both lost foothold. What a night to remember. While they climbed out, several female battleaxes stormed out of the hall muttering 'First Corinthians six, verse nine.' And even the most innocent knew what was implied—the war had started, the Tommies were in high demand and Hot Ruby had already had her 'wee lovebird'.

Tuesday evenings were secular and dedicated to C.L.B., the Church Lads' Brigade. It took many months to save up enough pennies to buy a uniform, though even then it was not completely mine. I went with the pennies, converted now into rare shillings, to the hall for the dark blue military-looking shirt and the peaked cap. A boiling nervousness bubbled inside me—such smart clothes carrying at once a sense of power and superiority and expressing the feeling of belonging to a body corporate, could not fail to rouse my strongest emotions. So pleased was I with the new acquisition that I dressed up in it and went down to the main road, so that I could stand to attention and salute when funerals went up to the cemetery, as I had seen soldiers do.

For youthful energies, many outlets were provided by the C.L.B. in gymnastics and boxing. Camping in the summer was available for those who could find twelve-and-sixpence, a sum of a magnitude quite beyond my comprehension. In any case I had humbler assignments elsewhere for living under canvas, and I did not particularly want to go to the C.L.B.

camps where eight o'clock bed was the rule. In the winter there were theatricals and displays of vaulting the horse and tumbling on large mats, given to a public audience.

A service in St. Anne's Cathedral was the year's climax, when the Church Lads from all over the city and beyond, from the scattered parishes of Down, Connor and Dromore, went to hear their bishop, Dr. MacNeice; and afterwards to parade round the cathedral. There in the gloaming on the great steps, crozier in hand, surrounded by masses of robed clergy, stood the magnificent bishop. But fear and trembling possessed me as I approached, for dread that my feet would go astray and be out of step and disgrace our company. The wife of our company's captain stood on the pavement, and she was known to note down the names of such defaulters. The bishop's own son, Louis, was not there, but was probably in Birmingham University putting down his poems of social protest.

Our theatrical repertoire was not extensive, and one winter we acted the story of *The Fourth Wise Man*. My mother being away at work, the neighbour who was looking after us sent me off with my sister's pink party dress, silk stockings and her own high-heel shoes, to play the part of a Roman slave-girl!

A service in the parish hall for the poorest children filled up Wednesday night. None of the Church Lads went except me, but then I preferred the rougher company found there, especially as a lantern lecture formed the backbone of the programme. We regarded it as going to the cinema, and were impatient for the lights to be put out and for the shaky pictures to be thrown on the screen. But the congregation was more often than not a mob of young toughs for whom the darkness invited every kind of devilry. At every other slide, the lights had to be put on again and admonitions given.

Throughout the week I contrived to get into some form

59

of entertainment, whether it bore a religious label or not. Anything in fact, to save me from going to bed. Some meetings served as alibis: I never went to all of them, especially when I was older. But I pretended I had, cloaking from my mother the fact that I had been keeping scores and chalking cues in the floating green twilight of the billiard saloons, or sitting in the tiny wooden shed where the pipe-band practised, deafening me with its screaming skirl.

We also enjoyed the church for its services, as well as its entertainments, especially for funerals and weddings, even outside the pin-hole season. Funerals had the additional attraction of lowered blinds to the street windows, when, suspecting a death, we would knock on the door and respectfully ask if we might see the coffin, although the family concerned might be completely unknown to us.

For weddings, of equal interest in our eyes, we adopted practices more in keeping with the joyful occasion. Squeezing in the crush after the service, we took up places near the bride and her attendants while they were being photographed. Our object was to pinch the bridesmaids' bottoms, creating (to us at any rate) an amusing diversion.

Despite my dreadful deeds during the week, I was content to get into my navy serge suit to go to Sunday School twice on Sundays, besides attendance at morning and evening service. No doubt the attraction was the eerie stories of the supernatural told by my teacher, the smart young man from the corner boot shop. Admittedly, a certain number of services was compulsory, for not only did I belong to the Church Lads' Brigade, but I was a parish orphan, one of that wretched corps obliged to patronize every church activity.

In our own house too were reminders of religion, not that my mother was 'saved'. She did not object to an odd bottle of stout if it was going, and made no bones about having a boy-friend. Nevertheless, not a wall but had its pictures, though nothing so popish as to include haloed humans. There was an immense one of the Lord's Prayer done in silver paper, the pious appliqué of one of the great-uncles. Hanging on either side of it, bunches of roses entwined with texts printed in squat gothic letters, and were framed in monstrous Victorian carving.

A schoolgirl on the wall over my bed was the exception to the rule of no figures; but she clutched a fat Protestant Bible, gazing up to riven clouds where a shaft of light pierced through; her eyes shone unbelievably moist. Printed on the cardboard mount underneath, now a little mottled and brown, was

> *My faith looks up to Thee,*
> *Thou Lamb of Calvary,*
> *Saviour divine.*

A prolonged struggle between my mother and me followed Uncle Hughie's gift of the 'Ceremony of Samurai', before I won a victory, and nailed it up next to the holy girl.

In the kitchen, where we lived, gothic lettering appeared again, this time with renderings of whole psalms, neatly done up in passe-partout. These more modern ones came from my mother's family, but the older ones in the frames with crossed corners, from my father's parents, who had been converted in late life at the Wee Mission. Although none of us was 'saved', to take the pictures down was more than we dared. We had similar ideas about good and bad luck over the torn pages of hymn-books and Bibles, which we never destroyed, but stacked away in the cupboard behind the gas-meter.

When autumn came, the barrier between conformity and dissent was torn down and all except the Mickeys went to the harvest thanksgivings in church and mission hall. The best of these, without doubt, was the Methodists'! At the end of the service there would always be 'testimonies'. I could

61

hardly wait for the succession of hymns, Bible readings, and sepulchral prayers to be over, so that the excitement of testimonies could begin. Old crones from the neighbourhood confessed to saving grace and you could always hope for a few piquant admissions of sin to add the *risqué* element of human shortcomings to the proceedings. It was never a good testimony unless some soul was laid bare, and lacerated with the scourging of self-confession. We derived much amusement from hearing a woman declare how many years she had been 'saved'. Though she would have died to own up in public that she was over fifty, she would be proud to admit that it was forty-two years since she had 'met the Lord'.

The tedium of the service itself was easily beguiled. Boys like myself emulated the older ones in seeing how many grapes and apples we could lay our hands on during the service. This was sometimes quite a number, as the sermon, in certain places, lasted upwards of an hour. While preacher thumped his Bible and ranted yet again about states of life in heaven and hell, surreptitious fingers would remove an apple and stow it away in a best-suit pocket. Having had more years of experience, the older boys were better at this. They could also spot the best positions in the mission hall the moment they got in the door; and they would go early to ensure a good, and fruitful, place. Such innocent faces gazed at the platform, but such artful fingers worked when the divine's countenance was directed to the other side of the room. Different districts did not all hold their thanksgiving on the same Sunday, so that in one season it was possible to attend quite a lot.

Besides the crowded Sunday services, the parish church that supported me had a Monday harvest thanksgiving as well, before the heaps and mounds of flowers and fruit were distributed. Cissy and I, of course, were there, our largest shopping-bags under the seat, for we were numbered among the needy. We had always strict instructions not to take home vegetable-marrows, they filled shopping bags but not stomachs. Our special aim was to get the lovely, crispy loaf, baked in the shape and size of a wheat-sheaf that stood on what we called the 'communion table'. The word 'altar' was never heard on our Protestant lips.

But the rector was more than generous in filling our cornucopia. He was a man with a huge voice that sought out every crack and corner of the church. Not much liked by my own family, he saved me, not from the 'wrath to come', but on endless occasions from approved schools; and I shall probably never reckon fully how much my life owed to him. From his house every Saturday morning, I collected the orphan money. But I remember him best on a Christmas Eve when I had to go up to the rectory for a joint provided by the parish poor-box. His wife handed me a parcel and off I went. But I did not get far before Ould Willie the rector came bawling after me. What was the good, he demanded, of that skinny piece of meat for four people, and made me go back for a heftier piece.

His parish was vast, much of it poor, but by a kind of sixth sense, Ould Willie knew the needs of everyone. My first appreciation came while I was in hospital where the curate came to visit me instead of the rector. The long-limbed young man in sombre clothes and glasses, could say nothing. We were worlds apart. When the silent awkward minutes had passed, he left, promising to send me copies of *Sunny Stories*. He never did; I knew Ould Willie would not have made such a promise and then broken it.

Not only did I swim in such a spate of public religion, but I evolved a secret salvation. From a date given in a Sunday School prize book I worked out that I must have first joined when three years old. Having been taught to say my prayers night and morning it occurred to me that for those three years of infancy there was a deficiency when I had said none. This loss had to be recuperated, and so I calculated the number of days in three years, and multiplied by two to get the requisite number of Our Fathers and family prayers. While munching a stolen apple maybe, or reading Orange slogans scrawled on public lavatories, I would mechanically gallop through my prayer debt at top speed.

And in a single year I would have heard about two hundred sermons, yet out of all the years and all the words, only two ever meant anything to me. The first was preached by the curate in the parish church, at my C.L.B. enrolment service—and his topic 'Clean Hands'. I pricked my ears up at this, for on his visits to me in hospital I had scrutinized his hands, clean and soft, resembling pale pork sausage meat. They were faintly revolting, so utterly different from my mother's, and certainly not a man's hands.

My mother's were the only other hands I knew closely, knobbly fingered, knotted with veins and sinews, completely patterned with black lines like the lead in a stained glass window, the nails bent and deformed from a piece of iron that fell on them, and not even the washing of twenty blankets would remove the lines of dirt embedded in the leathery palms. The skin was so roughened that it was like a dark hoar frost, but not one likely to be thawed by respite from work. Big 'Ina's hands were her hallmark. I stood beside her once as she was interviewed for a new job as char. 'And what references have you?' None, she had none except her hands and when asked if she was a good worker, she held them out. They were a living testimonial. I was so proud of them.

As the curate went on with his 'Clean Hands' I set about praying secretly, like a witch casting a spell, that he would stumble over his words. At his best he lacked fluency, and embarrassing pauses interrupted his discourse, when he adjusted his glasses and tried to find the place in his notes.

But the other sermon affected me differently. A crowd of children sat rapt before an evangelist in a hall near the Bog Meadows. Silence prevailed except for his voice and the ticking of a clock under which was printed 'Where will you spend eternity?'

Where indeed? Before this fiery Scot with his gutturals and growling r's came, we thought we should dwell in heaven with a God like Father Christmas, only white instead of red. But the preacher clearly held other views, God was in Belfast, in the very hall where we sat, and most amazing of all, out in the Bog Meadows among the tinkers' tents!

'God', he thundered as though selling a proprietary soap, 'is in the humblest tinker's home. . . .' And here his voice dropped, as if a gale had suddenly ceased, leaving the sea calm. Now he whispered sweetly through his teeth '. . . and so is wee Jaysus!'

'Amen, Brother. *Jehovah-Shammah*.' This interruption took the edge off the preacher's dramatic impact. It was the contribution from a bent man with a face like Punch, who peddled boot-laces and combs from door to door. His 'Amens, Hallelujahs, Jehovah-this-and-that' could not be repressed during any sermon he heard. If a hand went up showing a sinner was ready for salvation, the old pedlar became more voluble than the speaker.

Unperturbed, the Scottish preacher continued his idyll, 'Wee Jaysus was just one of you, poor laddie, wanting his tea before going to bed.'

Anthropomorphic, but appealing. Now we could dispense with God's lawn-sleeved nightshirt and wings, and concentrate on Jaysus of the tinkers' camp. How much better it was to pray to someone who smelt of a stable and wanted a bit of potato-bread for His tea!

Sermons went in one ear and out of the other, but not so the hymns. They lodged firmly somewhere between, their hymn-book numbers imprinting themselves on our brains. We could go into church or conventicle, see numbers up on a board and know by a kind of reflex action which hymns we were to have, or which selection from *Sacred Songs and Solos* or *Alexander's No.3*.

But the rousing choruses; the banal jigging of Moody and Sankey with their tedious modulations from tonic to dominant, from dominant to subdominant and so through to the inevitable perfect cadence; and the martial hymns of a church militant, left my soul unmoved. For singing and shouting in a fine release of feelings, choruses could not be bettered. For stamping feet and for the Church Lads' Brigade, the military hymns seemed to have been specially made. But music entered by another door, I knew nothing of music's sweetness until an old fiddler hopped along our entry on his wooden leg. Even then, the honeyed melodies, which years afterwards I knew to be from Italian operas, seemed more beautiful for issuing from the violin. It was a miracle.

I would hear the sound of it coming from somewhere between the yard walls; the operas were varied, by *The Old Rugged Cross* at some back doors if this would wring more coppers from the audience. Then he would reach our own part of the entry. And I, perched on the yard wall, marvelled that such music could come out of a fiddle. How did the agile bow manage such tricks? At one moment it flew to and fro like a shuttle weaving a sound pattern of the finest threads, and the next, rode purposefully up and down, like the prow of a ship cresting a rolling swell of melody. But the fiddle, how delicious it looked! The bellied wood glowed with the ripe reds of our Parrish's Chemical Food, mellowed by age to the rich tinge of Tate and Lyle's Golden Syrup.

More dreams than I ever dreamt about music lay in store. An Elder of the Open Plymouth Brethren collected old gramophone records. He used them as an artist's canvas and painted scenes on one side of them, appropriate to the subject, finishing his disc pictures off with a Biblical quotation. Then he would pass them on. To me he gave the *Hills of Donegal*, a sad, melancholy range of green, smeary hills painted across the tiny grooves, with, at the bottom, 'I will lift up mine eyes unto the hills'. It was my great treasure and when I heard the other side on the gramophone, something inside me seemed to melt, and flew out of me, to join with the velvet voice of Phyllis Lett. No voice ever thrilled or haunted me so much until, years after, I heard Kathleen Ferrier.

At that time, my supreme emotional experience compounded mystically of music and religion was when someone took me into St. George's church down town. The choir of boys, looking immaculate and pure in white surplices, sent icy pinnacles of sound into the dark roof. The beautiful precision of contrapuntal singing, the sweet agony of drawn-out chords, even to my untutored ears, was a finer thing than the cock-and-hen choirs (usually more hen than cock, and scrawny ones at that) of the familiar churches and mission halls nearer home.

The soul of music in our parish church so far as I was concerned, lay within the great organ. I admired its ranks of pipes, the slim architecture of a heavenly city. After my discovery of music its magnificence put even the red fleur-de-lys curtains to shame. How I longed to master those white banks of stops, waiting like grapes in the harvest thanksgivings to be plucked by the handful; how my feet itched to flit over the obedient, throaty pedals, and my fingers to race over the tiered keyboards. But my enthusiasm was not enough to carry me far on the road to fame.

The only success I ever had in church music was as a stage-prop. By oversight or mistake someone included me in a children's choir giving a concert. But at the final rehearsal a new music teacher appeared on the scene. She initiated a witch-hunt to track down the out-of-tune voice which threatened to wreck the whole performance. 'Too strong', she pronounced my voice to be, having identified me as the culprit. All attempts to control it proved vain, and she only allowed me to stay on condition that no sound issued out as I stood mouthing the words. News of my humiliation spread like wild-fire round the congregation, and I felt that all eyes were riveted on the mummer during the recital. No wonder I experienced greater musical fulfilment in the gospel hall, where the louder the better was the password, and no inhibitions at all could be suffered as a chorus boy singing,

I am H-A-P-P-Y,
I am H-A-P-P-Y,
I know I am,
I'm sure I am,
I am H-A-P-P-Y.

Tinker, Tailor, Soldier, Sailor

When the Old Soldier came in his shabby black overcoat to the wooden hut near our house I felt the first pangs of ambition. I too wanted to be a night-watchman. It was evening when he arrived. The men had dug a fine large hole in the road, and were stacking their picks and shovels in the hut. For me, to begin work when other people had finished and were on their way home to supper and bed was something special. With my nose pressed against the cold glass of the bedroom window, I watched him move about, now in shadow, now in light, settling for the night. The glow of his fire, suggesting the cosy depths of his hut, was too strong a temptation, and after being sent to bed, I escaped out of the house to share in the Old Soldier's wonderful life.

And what a life, perfect in every detail. Nobody was there to worry him about bedtime, or washing, or homework, or dull food. When he was tired, as if anyone would be in those circumstances, he simply put his feet up on the planks and went to sleep. But equally, he could sit through the forbidden hours of darkness peering into the rose flames of his brazier. He had never to think of being clean, and because there was nowhere to wash, his hands were always comfortably dirty. And if he was hungry, then out came the newspaper with hunks of cheese and new bread, the brazier was stoked and piled with showers of coke, and the tea-can set singing on top like a cage of canaries. His hut was the ideal house, not full of furniture and useless ornaments that fell and broke every time you touched them. Along the sides were plank seats held up on bricks, and at the end stood a big wooden box full of tarpaulins, tools and coils of rope, and that was all. The smell was a healthy and strong one of pitch and oil.

To show that this roadside life had order and meaning, a nightly routine was followed. It began with building up the brazier and coaxing the green and violet deep in its heart, with dead ashes raked in a little pyramid on the ground underneath. Then came the grand climax, the lighting and setting out of the hurricane lamps. They were marshalled on the ground near the entrance to the hut, those with red glass in one row and those with clear glass in another. Paraffin was poured carefully into each, and the little screw cap put on again. The glass was raised and the fringe of wick touched with a burning taper.

In princely procession, with a lamp in each hand, the Old Soldier and I walked into the growing darkness, shining like the first created stars. By the barrier of trestles and scaffold poles round the hole, or by the heaps of earth that had come out of it, the warning lamps were spaced out. The Old Soldier went out and trimmed them later on in the night when, as he put it, he was the only mortal thing awake.

For the local boys and girls, the Old Soldier kept open house. I was much younger than the others who were all allowed to stay up, but nobody minded. We sat on the plank benches, our faces tingling from the fire, excited into silence by adventure tales of the Old Soldier's early life. Halfway through a story he would stop, leaving a soldier in the Boer war behind a rock with the enemy in front and a lion behind, to make tea as black as treacle, and sweeter than anything you ever imagined. From a treasure tin, with a lid at each end, he took out the tea and sugar, the hopeful eyes of his visitors following every movement. Not one would presume to ask, but all knew that on the coldest nights there would be a long warming pull at the chipped blue and white enamel mug.

Then the story would be taken up again, and looking into his bleary eyes where they shone from deep recesses above hoary white-whiskered cheeks, I saw the wide world unfold. It was a vision of the Veldt, and of polished brass buttons and helmets, spiralling puttees, the tap of drums, of glinting swords, and horses galloping across grassy plains trundling great cannons.

'God-Save-The-Queen', the Old Soldier would exclaim, and jump up to see who was turning out the red lamps, or what drunkard's voice was calling for help from the bottom of the hole. With this one and only swear word, the story was left again, its hero in a worse predicament than before.

The Boer war business might have happened on the moon for all we knew until the Old Soldier took us on his campaigns. We idolized him for he had got his stripes in the Mileeshy— the real South Down Militia, the greatest regiment ever. How justifiably he could boast:

When Kruger heard the regiment was landed in Capetown,
'De Wet,' says he 'we're lost.' Says he, 'They've sent out the
    South Downs.'
Says De Wet, 'If that's a fact, me son, we'd better quit the Rand,
For them South Down Mileeshy is the terror of the land.'

When at the Jubilee the Irish Rifles they marched by,
Her Majesty observed them with a keen and martial eye
'Och, Major Wallace,' says the Queen, 'Thim boys of yours looks
    grand.'
'Och, hould your tongue,' says Wolseley, 'Thim's the terror of the
    land.'

Tinker, Tailor, Soldier, Sailor

Romantic night-life as lived by the Old Soldier seemed the ideal existence for a time. Then farming came to my notice. I deserted from the army ranging the Veldt and gave my loyalty to new dreams. In school, our teacher brought the branch of an apple tree, and from it hung two beautiful apples, ripe and fresh-cheeked. I had never seen an apple tree before; orchards and blossom had not come within my experience, only the frog-hunting days in the Bog Meadows. But now a new wonder filled me, I would become a farmer and live among such trees. And this ambition was encouraged by a stuffed squirrel who sat on the top of our classroom cupboard. I never tired of watching it, and of waiting for a sly moment to stroke its back. For all that, its eye never winked, nor did the brown, silky body dart away with the acorn, held between front paws.

And on Fridays, when the dustbin men came round the entries collecting refuse, I dearly longed to be one of them. What treasures they were for ever picking up. What marvels could be found in the bins of wealthy homes up the Malone Road, where women took their baths in milk and the men had winter vests of ermine. Charlie Price, three doors down from us, was on the bins. He had brought home a plaster bust of some really big-wig (it was actually Wagner) from his refuse round. That was an object on one's parlour mantelpiece worth boasting about—so different from the conch shells and inevitable clocks shaped like Napoleon's hat. Let stuck-up neighbours say what they would, to be on the bins was more exciting than their grand husbands' dull jobs as winding-masters, stevedores, coppersmiths or yarndressers.

Although I shelved each ambition as a new one appeared, and had definitely rejected the night-watchman's career, I never forgot the tales of the Old Soldier's roaring South African youth. But the nearest I could get to those vanished days was in a taxidermist's, down off the main square. Two decrepit brothers sat decaying amidst moth-eaten heads mounted on wooden shields, stuffed cats in glass cases, stiff mummified birds, a dog with no tail, and in one corner a whole lion slowly dropping to pieces. But the shop made Africa real, and clothed the Old Soldier's stories in the glamour of truth.

And in the doctor's waiting-room too, where I loved to be left alone when a visit was necessary, another thrill waited. In front of the fire lay a magnificent leopard skin, the head complete with eyes and snarling mouth. I used to get down, making sure that no one was coming, and putting my mouth near the animal's, touch the fierce fangs with my tongue, and gently rub my cheek up and down the soft fur. 'Bet I've done something you haven't,' I could show off to my friends, 'put my tongue in a leopard's mouth.'

To see these things for myself leaping and snarling in their jungles, then became urgent and a new ambition ousted the others. I wanted to go, not as hunter, but as missionary.

In church and mission hall alike, missionaries were most popular. They trailed honour and glory behind them, and a complement of more invitations to tea with church ladies than could ever be accepted. Some atmosphere of a sacrificial victim clung about them. They were always at pains to make everyone aware of how much Christ had demanded of them, and of the comfortable lives at home and future prospects they had given up—for Him. The effect on the audience was to make them thoroughly conscious of complacency and laziness. Not all of course, were called to brave swamps and deserts, but a flood of pennies would do much to compensate those who had been. Why was it that the rector or resident ministers did not feel acutely embarrassed as they listened to stay-at-home cowards being denunciated? But of course, the missionaries' careful elaboration of their sacrifices was a hysterical cover-up of the fact that life at home had become so dreary and 'the field' offered excitements otherwise unobtainable.

However, we crushed into their 'Valedictory Services' announced on posters as 'Life in the Field', 'The Labourers are Few', 'The light in Darkest Africa', in a receptive, not a critical mood. Achievements, not motive, was the big draw. No bishop, hair-raising evangelist, or even the ex-boxer minister who suddenly shouted in the middle of his exegesis and made the old ladies jump and mutter 'Oh dear!' to their friends, none of these could compare with a missionary. Desert sand still clung to their shoes, the steam of tropical forests had hardly dried out of their clothes, and the chatter of heathen tongues was still louder in their ears than the choruses of the congregation at home.

Brave men, willing to risk all! How I would have jumped at the opportunity to go! Purely on a basis of expenditure and return, the number of converts naturally formed their principal theme, the greater the number then obviously the more successful they had been. You had to accept that with missionaries—whether they were 'sprinklers' on the black heathen foreheads only, or thorough 'plungers' by total immersion in alligator-infested rivers. But when all the claptrap was over, they got down to the heart of their sermon, the travelogue part, though perhaps with a last interruption while a wife sang 'Jesus loves me, this I know' in an African dialect. A pity, we thought, since many of these wives were fat, that they never told us of attempts to push them into a cooking pot. Finally clear of all the nonsense, the missionaries could proceed with the principal business of thrilling episodes of ambush, journeyings by canoe over rapids, the risk of poisoned arrows and barbed spears, and countless perils of death from disease and hostile jungle.

About this time, I saw a film of Stanley going out to meet

Livingstone, and my ambition to be a missionary was confirmed. The young explorer, at the head of a long queue of the 'black folk' bearing his luggage on their heads, pushed ahead through the pampas-grass. Behind him, the bearers were singing 'Onward Christian Soldiers'. At the end of the film, when he found the old missionary, a feast was called for, and the young black boys scurried round chasing Livingstone's piglets to catch and cook them.

Then one day, I discovered a dilapidated tin-roofed building about a mile from our house. It was filled with blue and yellow smoke that sometimes hung about inside, or billowed out into the street, carrying a strange smell of burning unlike anything else I had known. The first time, I stood enraptured for hours listening to the unsuspected music of clanging anvil, watching the patient horses with glistening bodies lift up a hoof, which smoked so terribly when the searing shoe was put on.

The blacksmiths then were lords of creation for me, did they not own the most marvellous fire in the world? Sophie's hundred-eyes out in the Bog Meadows was not in the same class, nor were the dancing amethyst sylphs of the Old Soldier's brazier. The blacksmith's fire spluttered like a firework display, shedding sparklers of burning red, while its anthracite heart became as brassy and yellow as our front-door knocker after its Saturday cleaning. It was a smooth, sleek, fierce fire crouching under the iron chimney, its red-hot eyes glowing like the tigers I imagined in the jungle. Mine were trembling hands indeed that the blacksmith allowed to pump the bellows. Every day I was there standing, oblivious of the heat, working the gasping bellows up and down. Without any doubt, I wanted to be apprenticed along with the sweat-shining, muscle-bound youths in dirty singlets and torn leather aprons, who thrust the shoes and turned them in the heart of the fire.

Tinker, Tailor, Soldier, Sailor

Not far from the forge I found a very puzzling affair, a stone horse-trough with a singing cistern and clear, beautiful water. Yet we were forbidden to drink from it, in spite of the chiselled gothic lettering on the side, 'Ho, every one that thirsteth, come ye to the waters'. Surely old Mary, the bread-server's heavy mare, could not read it? It seemed strange that people did not clamber into the trough and have a good, swanky bath, instead of fighting over whose turn was next in the small tin tub before the kitchen fire.

Before long, I had joined a gang and they took me beyond our streets, through the pompous suburbs, to green fields and woods, and the banks of the river Lagan. Here, where the barges glided rust-red through the still waters, lay a new world. Sitting spellbound on Shaw's Bridge, I watched the tow-ropes slacken and tauten, and waited for the horse. There were weirs, and the horses had to cross from one side of the river to the other. I saw dogs sleeping on the bows, and bare-footed boys running round, whistling their carefree days away. Was it possible that these people really lived with no need of land or houses? And unbelieving, I watched them go under the ancient bridge. Although I never forgot the Old Soldier or the blacksmiths, a life on land even with hut and brazier, anvil and smoking hooves, was not to be thought of. I wanted to go to sea.

As I grew older the new ambition filled my life. Poetry homework from school could be devoured now for it was 'Cargoes'. None of us could possibly pronounce such perverse words as 'Quinquireme of Nineveh', but nevertheless, gleams of a golden life beyond my own city and beyond my own time came from my magical combination of words and ships. The evocative effect of harbour and verse now became richer than even that of the missionaries' 'From Greenland's icy mountains'.

I often forsook the gang and braved alone the suburbs and

began to haunt the wharves and quaysides miles away from home. The cross-channel steamers tied up here, and cradled between the steel gantry bulrushes, the shells of warships, crustaceous and curvilinear, lay grey against a grey sea. And perhaps great four-masted barques of the Australian grain races probed the sky with a forest of spars and rigging, as I wandered up and down, drinking deep at the sight of ships.

In dreams, I was the captain of each in turn, keeping the rising and falling bow on course during a storm, or nosing capably to berth after a successful voyage round the world. In reality, I stood on the very edge of the quayside and touched the steel sides as if they belonged to me, and gazed giddily down where the rusty anchor plunged into the water. By the time I was eleven I knew every boat that came in, their numbers and the meanings of the colourful patterned funnels. The cold touch of their sides was a link with faraway places, and with the grey rolling sea between me and Uncle Hughie's 'Great Gate of Nikko', the glitter of Sauchiehall Street, the sandalwood and sweet white wine from distant Ophir.

And over the wet cobbles of the quayside came the ringing of boots, the music of pleasure-hunting seamen, whose swarthy looks and heathen language would have put Mrs. Patterson, who prayed in 'tongues' at queer Second Blessing halls, out of the count.

Desire was whetted by these visits, and when the frustration of being a landlubber was bearable no longer, my venture was decided. I had to feel a deck and the sea's swell under my feet, or die. The channel steamers made trips along the coast, setting off on Sunday mornings, and returning the same night. Tickets were not exorbitant, measured against the thrill they provided, and a careful working out of makes and wings could buy one. Deserted buildings were always waiting to be gutted which could be sold as firewood, somebody's greyhound needed exercising, or a neighbour wanted my extra-long legs, for me to whitewash the kitchen ceiling, and if all else failed I might steal a few wings from Big 'Ina.

The problem was to evade home and my mother, for she would neither understand nor approve my going to sea, even if only for the day on Sunday. But it was unthinkable to forgo the trip, or even to share it. The supreme moment of departure could not be tarnished by parental cautions about leaning over the side, or getting in the sailors' way. There were certain things a man's soul had to face alone, and this was one.

A plan came quickly enough, having made the decision and the necessary shilling to go. Because it was summer, I could go away camping on the Saturday, but return to the city early on Sunday morning to board the boat, so that Big 'Ina would never know.

Saturday evening was interminable, and in the night chill of the tent it seemed that Sunday's dawn would never come. But it did eventually, fine, and too clear, with the distance drawn in fine detail. The booking-office had not opened when I got down to the quayside, and I was first in the queue. With great self-confidence I pushed my money through the window when a bald man opened it at nine o'clock. Then I ran to the waiting gangway and went up almost in one leap. It was happening, I was aboard my first ship. I had gone to sea!

The moment of touching the deck became fixed, like the resin of primeval forests changed to amber. A sailor, passing along with an oil-can and oily rags, winked at me, and the shadow of a swooping gull darted over the scrubbed decks and spotless white paint. A ship farther down the quayside sent out a hoot which echoed between the warehouses as though looking for a place to rest and finding none. The man collecting tickets tore mine in half down its dotted line, and the loudspeakers relayed music. The little accidents of that moment were caught fast and then released in the stream of time again, like a floating twig held by weeds before being swept onwards.

I had bought a paper hat, and so had some of the other trippers in frivolity. But mine was a symbol of vocation, made of paper only because I was not old enough for a real one. Nevertheless it was a success with the factory girls out for the day, and before we were in the channel, I had friends amongst the crew. I explored every corner of the ship and was allowed down to the engine-room hissing with pent-up power. After an hour I knew my way round as well as the streets of our neighbourhood. Then I took up a position right in the bow, looking down at the peeling, frothing water I had watched so often from the shore.

We steamed slowly by the dun-tinted mudflats beloved of the waders, on past the reclaimed lands and silent dredgers hung with buckets like church bells in a steeple. Northwards, the noble basalts of Antrim rose up in blues and blacks, with the sleek folds of ermine breakers clinging about their rugged feet. But on the south side—the side where I was born amid the bare cathedral gantries—spread the soft hills of Down with bearded woods turning to autumnal sleep.

But the morning's brightness proved to be treacherous, clouds flew across the sky, and driving rain sent the mill girls squealing below to make eyes at possible dancing partners and sing 'South of the border down Mexico Way'. Drenched through, I clung to the rail, thrilled at an encounter with the sea in a not-so-kind mood. Behind the streaming saloon windows I could see the blur of dancers, and above the slap of the waves wailed the dance band. Well pleased with the wildness of the sea, I threw away the soggy remains of the sailor hat, and went in to see the fun.

A girl standing near the door looked me up and down and

asked how old I was. Fourteen, I lied, and this served her
purpose for she was sulking from her boy-friend. She used me
to show how well she could get on without him, and invited
me to go out to a sheltered part of the deck. When the boy-
friend came out, to annoy him the girl pretended to make
love by trying to guillotine my tonsils with her tongue. It had
the desired effect, she was pulled roughly away, and the hot,
scented kiss was replaced by a stubbly chin scraped up and
down my tender cheeks, to teach me a lesson.

And all too soon night turned our boat about, and the moon
was up. Its reflection rode the growing waves like a silver
cascade of Honiton lace. Stomachs that had survived the sea's
motion during the rain and wind, now capitulated to the
evening tide. Drunkards and abstainers alike lined the rails
heaving and retching. A mood of abstraction induced by my
first day at sea, possessed me still, and the ship's irregular
movement was for me nothing but its breathing.

At least, until someone slapped me on the back. I thought
the blow would send me over into the waves which I so
feared and so greatly loved. Recovering balance, I turned to
see who my hearty friend could be. Shivers ran in my spine
and my heart ran in a rhythm contrary to the ship's. It was
Joe, a lodger beside us at home, a cobbler by trade, and an
admirer of Big 'Ina. There was no longer any question that
she would know of my sea adventure, before I climbed the
stairs that night.

Then suddenly Joe flung himself at the rail, and the hot
beery stench hit me, borne on the wind. A queer feeling in-
vaded my legs and acid saliva ran in my mouth and as I joined
company with the others at the rail, Joe and my mother's
punishment ceased to matter. And my elaborate fantasies
about barges on the Lagan and galleons on the Spanish Main
sank to the bottom of my mind's sea. In drab misery, only a
longing for the lights of Belfast remained, and for the firm

Tinker, Tailor, Soldier, Sailor

granite of earthbound streets, and my own steady bed where
my last thoughts would be thanks that

> *Home is the sailor, home from sea,*
> *And the hunter home from the hill.*

Down by the Sally-Bushes

A make on the line, they said, always became a wing.

But for once they were wrong.

Clutching the precious halfpenny I ran through the long grass, expecting to find the ground slippery and wet, and hidden among tall tufts, the carcasses of dead dogs and cats thrown over the palings and barbed wire. Now I was on the other side myself, defying the iron notice board used for catapult practice, that by its 'Trespassers will be prosecuted' seemed connected in some way with the Lord's Prayer.

Taking leaps down the slope, I thought of all the times I had wanted to climb the palings and of the envy I suffered when other boys talked of exploits along the railway verges. Now I had done it. Scaling the wood sleeper fence had been easier than I imagined, and below for the first time lay the shining river of steel, that issued from the city on one side, but on the other flowed into eternity.

The signals gave a warning click, and the wires that pulled them like puppets, sang metallically and were still again. Close to, the rails were bigger than I thought, wider apart, the sleepers and gravel making a heavenly highway, leading out from the streets and factory chimneys to the green beyond. But there was no time to dream. My ears detected a distant rumble. A train! Quickly and carefully I placed my make on the top flange of the rail and retired to the cover of the long grass.

Down by the Sally-Bushes

Soon I would see the transformation. When the train had gone, I would dash over and collect the pressed-out wing.

Then it appeared, not too slow, not too fast, heavy, muscled with power, trailing its own clouds, that wreathed and whirled, and finally melted into the sky. The distance lessened between the engine's relentless wheels and my little make. The music now, of steam and iron, made a thousand crescendos. Trumpets of high-pressure steam sounded from the black belly, and were drowned by the clank and rumble of invincible drummers, hammering out the mighty sounds of metal on metal. My eyes followed the giant wheels' counter-weights as they rose and fell over the place where my half-penny lay.

Carriage wheels ran over the coin then, singing a lighter song. And when the guard's van slipped by, and began to grow smaller, and the noise ceased to burst like rockets in my ears, I came out from hiding, and went to see how well my new wing was minted. Picking up the deformed coin, I was disappointed. The transformation had not been so miraculous after all. The make had certainly increased in diameter, but could not really be called a convincing penny.

But I had no real regrets; for my first time on the forbidden railway property I had not done badly. And the whole experiment had been performed with the slot-machine for penny chocolate bars in mind. I wasted no more time, but put the new wing in my pocket, scrambled over the palings again, and dashed off to the slot-machine. The red machine had already devoured an assortment of foreign coins. These had been brought home by Grandpa from his years as a soldier. They found their way into Big 'Ina's sewing bag, where they kept company with hundreds of buttons. some of which were Grandpa's regimental ones.

Having been cheated before of pennies by an empty machine, I first looked through the glass for the pile of chocolate bars, before pushing my expanded make into the slot. The miracle wing went in and made a clattering sound inside. I pulled at the tray at the bottom, but it would not open. A bang on the front, a shake, a taking of the narrow red painted shoulders, but all to no avail. The railway wing had failed me.

And then the angel of the Lord appeared. 'Can I help you, little man?' It was Sister Winnie, the woman who came round the hospital singing hymns on Sunday with a pathetic soprano effect fifty years out of tune. But I got my wing, a whole genuine one out of her handbag, and this ample compensation cured my disappointment over the cripple in the machine.

Not long after my first invasion of the railway lines, I scrambled over the fence again. Though not for the intention of Stock Exchange dealings with makes and wings. Being ten years old now, I had outgrown the playing of shops in the entries, and had wearied of the doctor's role in the cobbled, entry hospitals. I wanted a man's life of roaming and adventure. And it could be found, I knew, along the railway. Our own side of the track was narrow and within range of the houses. But the farther side was very wide, secretive with sally-bushes and guarded by a steep incline. Something of a Japanese garden clung about the shadowy cloisters of the sally-bushes. They were thick enough to screen us from the world's prying eyes, dense enough to shut out the distant clanging of trams.

It was Gandhi's territory. His disciples gathered there to meet their leader, he whose shaved head and thin body belied the spiritual strength of his lion heart. But although Gandhi of the sally-bushes resembled his Indian namesake in many ways, he was a prophet of the devil, sitting crossed-legged as he flicked out the devil's emblems—hearts and diamonds, spades and clubs. I knew his notoriety before I knew him, and of the card-playing which even my mother would not have in the house. She winked her eye if a bottle of stout appeared, but at cards never—the mission hall's work was well done in that respect.

Gandhi ruled, a benevolent despot, and nature had designed him to do so. To me he seemed a terrible figure, stronger, older, wiser, braver than myself. True, he had reached puberty at a biologically remarkable early age and bore the stamp of manhood on his slender buttocks in the form of a star neatly tattooed on each side. But he still had to attend school like the rest of us, and must therefore have been under fourteen. He had ruled the gang for many years before the girls began to titter and make sly remarks about his extraordinary growth of hair. His head was shaved, of course, but only at certain seasons of the year when he needed a haircut. Then his father, a man loaded with a vast porter-belly, would get out his cut-throat and 'give him the works'.

I sought out the gang deliberately, crossing the lines on an afternoon when the trains seemed to be dashing by every minute, to do so. What I proposed doing was dangerous, but at that particular time life seemed to offer no alternative. When I asked to join the gang the boys would most probably attack and maim me in the way that Mickeys were said to. Older than myself, the boys came from the rougher streets, one and all were 'bad' and had been 'in trouble' officially.

Determination drove me on in spite of fear. I was sick of other company, soft boys from my own street who liked to play cricket, or listen to Children's Hour on the radio. And in any case a reputation for badness was already mine, why should I not have the fun as well as the blame? For so long now I had been told I was a scoundrel, wicked, a rogue, a dirty bugger, a liar into the bargain, and had all the 'makin's of a real bad one'. Most of this (not the dirty bugger) emanated from the great-aunts, but their evil propaganda began to

influence other people into similar beliefs. The strain of pre-
tending to be good was weighing on me. I wanted to be free
and become myself. If Gandhi would have me, I would throw
my lot in with him, burn my fingers on hell's cards, and have
done with struggling for appearances' sake.

Going straight up to Gandhi and asking outright if I might
join, was more than I could summon courage for. Instead I
hung about near their haunt, hoping to draw the attention of
Rusty Foster. Rusty and I had been in hospital together, and
both attended the tuberculosis clinic on Mondays. But Rusty,
conspicuous by the flaming hair that gave him his name, was
not at all anxious to be known as my friend among the sally-
bushes. Surprisingly, Gandhi himself made the opening move.

'Got any good butts?'

In reply I took out my cigarette case, an ex-mustard tin,
and extracted a beauty, nearly three-quarters of a whole fag.
Such luck often came my way, for Saturday afternoons were
devoted to beachcombing in the long dark tunnel under the
grand stand at the football stadium. The butt-end impressed
Gandhi, it opened the door to the gang. I was in, but only just
in. Before I could sit with the elect inhaling butt nicotine as
the fearful cards swished, swished in games played for high
stakes of matchsticks, a novitiate must be served.

This did not consist of ceremonies of initiation, but simply
of waiting hand and foot on the gods as they played at cards.
Potatoes had to be fetched and roasted in the camp-fire ashes.
And when the fire burned low, I ran along the rail tracks
collecting pieces of coal fallen from passing engines. Easier
fuel than coal, which could not always be found, was to remove the wooden blocks inserted under the rail. On that
first day, I so wanted to give a good account of myself to
Gandhi, that I carried many more of the blocks than the fire
demanded. The spare ones grew in a stack near the fire, like
peat out in the bogs.

Down by the Sally-Bushes

At home that night, as I sat staring at my school homework, the day's glories went in cavalcade before my inward eye. And then as a train thundered by, shaking the house, I thought of the wooden blocks. Icy fingers of fear groped at my heart. I had visions of a catastrophe and could hear the shuddering brakes. The death of passengers was not my fear so much as that perhaps the derailed engine might crash into our house lying close by. When darkness hid everything but the winking signal lights, I went back to replace the left-over blocks we had not burnt. The sound of knocking reached the ears of the law, and I escaped only because I could climb barbed wire more nimbly than policemen.

Soon it became clear that my life could not be given both to school and the gang, and no doubt ever occurred as to which it should be. Mitching from school had to be launched on a grand scale, for many of the gang's plans involved climbing aboard the cattle-wagons of the railway, and travelling out of town for many miles. But time spent in travelling was not wasted, for the playing cards went too. In the wagon, dim and still redolent of cows' dung, the gang sat in a circle, flipping down the aces.

Either side of the Malone Road stood the larger houses of the wealthy where I went pin-holing. Among them were empty ones, sometimes derelict, hidden behind overgrown jungles of brambles and evergreen shrubbery. Their windows had long ago been broken and had fallen in, and loose blinds flapped or tapped eerily in the wind. Of these houses, one was reputed to be haunted. Before joining the gang I never ventured farther than its grounds. In spring, rhododendron blooms waited to be raped, and in autumn Michaelmas-daisies fell to the young intruder. I kept my eyes and ears open for any signs of a ghost, and would fly for life if a branch cracked or the wind moaned through the mouldy rooms. Everyone believed that the mad wife had come back as a ghost, to haunt the husband for ill-treating her, forcing him to abandon their old home.

But trespassing with the older boys was different, ghosts held no terrors for the gang, though they were great believers in the supernatural. Of the wife's madness not one of them was in doubt, and often speculated as to which part of the house had held her, like Rochester's wife, confined. When energetic enough to walk out there, plenty of fun could be had scampering from room to room, smashing the remaining windows, playing with the heaps of bottles and bits of broken furniture, hiding in the capacious cupboards.

'Gandhi! 'ere', an excited voice would shout from an upstairs room, and we all raced to the voice. 'Look at that. Bullet holes!' We craned to see the evidence of where the man had tried to shoot her. The interest of trying to piece together the mystery of the house never palled, and we were always finding marks on the walls to interpret as bullet holes, knife marks, or sinister smears of dried blood.

In the desolate kitchen, where thick wallpaper drooped and fungi grew on the ceiling, we found a table that puzzled us—before we finished it off by chopping it into firewood. A round hole in the centre was the puzzle; we could not discover its purpose. Finally we decided that though the house had a bathroom, the rich retained a few primitive feelings and had liked to squat up on the kitchen table. Another solution, more suited to our mood, was that the curious table formed another terrible torture instrument, which the man had used on his wife.

Speaking tubes ran through the house, and I felt sure, even when with the gang, that they were really haunted; it may have only been the wind, but they seemed to whisper orders for a downstairs staff long since departed. Apart from the marble bath, and its elaborate mahogany case, which still bore scratch marks, we fancied, from the unfortunate woman's struggle to avoid having her head pushed under the water, the best feature in the house was the food lift. Being the youngest and smallest, it was usually me who was crammed into the small cabinet and hoisted by the ropes up and down to the various floors. I loved it, until one day, during a pause in our cries, strange footsteps were heard below. Mighty dread seized us. The others fled, down the stairs, out of the windows, through the back door.

All escaped except me, for I was jammed at the bottom of the lift shaft, unable to get out. A prescient silence reigned in the house. Then the footsteps, cautious, unhurrying, advanced a little over the floor above. The floorboards creaked. Another dreadful pause. Chilled to the marrow, I knew the spectre was the mad woman come back to get me for climbing on the old kitchen table and making a mock of her agonies. The lift rope trembled; the most terrible moment of my life was upon me. Then, the steps retraced the same route, and ceased altogether.

A little afterwards, one of the gang poked his head in the lift and said it had only been Fat Pat, a detective whom we all knew. I never again volunteered for rides in the lift. A dislike of the place, that lurked at the back of my mind, now came to the fore. And it was not entirely because of my belief in ghosts. A worse terror haunted me—that the gang, through so much talk about the mad woman, would discover that dread sentence on my own father's death certificate. To cover up, I tried to exceed the others' mockery. Whenever possible I avoided going out to the house.

It was Fat Pat who had hunted me down in the first of my serious conflicts with authority. There was a strip of waste land at the back of a factory, which the gang occasionally visited to take away thrown-out wooden cases for firewood.

One day I took an extra large packing-case and sold it for

a penny to a neighbour who made cheap furniture. But that penny cost me dear, and almost the end of my freedom. With a savagery akin to the transportation laws of the 18th century, the company pursued the matter of their missing packing-case. Tired of the gangs who appropriated their waste land, they put the police on our trail. The box was traced to the furniture dealer, and Fat Pat eventually appeared on our doorstep.

I was eleven years old. The company insisted that justice should be done. In my defence the rector made much of the fact that I had no father, and that of necessity my mother was out working all day and much of the night. For days, my fate hung in the balance, but in the end, the company withdrew the charges. The directors summoned me to appear before them for the purpose of a very severe reprimand, an occasion thought suitable for the wearing of my C.L.B. uniform.

I cannot remember whether I had to give them their penny back.

The gang's outrages soon reached my mother's ears, ears that tingled already with my own individual crimes. My behaviour distressed her, and she like the rector was constantly saving me from approved school hands. Amongst the worst of my bad habits was that of visiting other people's houses, uninvited. A mixture of motives lay behind this, not always the desire to take things which I thought we should have, but sometimes to savour a luxury denied in our small home. Perhaps it was only curiosity or bravado.

Houses were irresistible. I was quick to notice if newspapers were used instead of tablecloths, or the milk bottle instead of a jug. I found it important to know if the beds were made and the po emptied, for to be as respectable as some of our neighbours fancied themselves, especially the 'saved' ones, the bed most certainly had to be made every day.

In the room of a house I once broke into, I found a bright

Down by the Sally-Bushes

chromium-plated lavatory chain with a vermilion rubber ball as a handle. How exciting it would be in our dreary W. C. in place of the piece of string that was for ever breaking! I duly installed it, to my mother's horror, for she knew at once I had pinched it. Down came the chain, and out came the thick leather strap that had been my father's shaving strop. I was strong, and a bully despite my cadaverous cheeks, but still no match for Big 'Ina who led me with great wallops, chain and red ball in hand, back to the owner to apologize.

When rain swamped the sally-bushes and frost was speared on the blades of grass, the gang moved headquarters to a disused chimney shaft on waste land near the river, for it could fight everything except winter. And in a bitterly cold spell, we were driven to a derelict mill. Within weeks we had ripped up hundreds of feet of floorboards, which we used as firewood, both to keep our own shins warm and to sell. The police must have missed us from the usual places and flung their net as far as the mill, but always too soon or too late. In the end their patrols increased, and we abandoned the building and returned to the chimney.

Huddled together at its base, we watched the icy disc of sky overhead, longing for signs of warmer weather. We sang ' 'Twas on the Isle of Capri that I met her', varied with 'She'll be coming round the mountain', and 'Red sails in the sunset' for more sentimental moments. Stones were at the ready for sleek rats running up the river bank, and eyes were kept open for male intruders who were warned off with choice threats of torture, including such standbys as the Chinese haircut and Red Indian burn. Females hardly received better treatment. Should one of us relieving himself be discovered by an occasional woman out exercising a greyhound, it was customary to shout 'Like to shake the crystals, Missus?' All too often they were ladies and pretended to ignore us, but sometimes they would shout angrily back 'I'm goin' straight to the barracks.

Down by the Sally-Bushes

You see if I don't—filthy bugger!' Only the boldest of girls ventured our way, near enough to be passionately devoured.

Our life was not always one of shades, lived furtively in disused buildings or on the railway verges. Glamour and bright lights played their part too. Hours brimful of excitement passed in amusement arcades where, dazzled by the sparkle, dazed by the whirl and speed, we found our heaven. It had angels too, the cheeky, highly-painted dolls, only a few years older than us, who walked between the rows of slot-machines with little leather change-bags.

And compared with other gangs we were not really bad, at least not in the sense that we carried out major raids, as did Tulip's gang which met farther up the line. We indulged only in petty thieving usually to keep the sally-bush larder supplied, to supplement cinema funds or buy cheap bangles for the girls in the arcades. At least, this was so in Gandhi's day. But the time came for Gandhi to leave us. He had retained leadership for a while, after leaving school and during the time when he tried to learn his father's trade of linenlapper.

But one day he said, quite suddenly, 'I'm takin' the king's shillun.'

His secret was out now. We knew the reason for his cooling off towards our wilder schemes, and for the distant look in an eye that before gleamed fire and murder. It was only too true, sure enough Gandhi went off as a band-boy in the army. I thought I understood—even the world of the sally-bushes had grown too small for Gandhi, just as the games of the entries had ceased, long before, to satisfy me. Gandhi's burning spirit was a bird grown tired of its cage, beyond the bars new horizons appeared. Our trusty leader had reached man's estate. Before he left we all trooped down to Bertie's tattoo saloon to see a parting memento engraved on his arm—the red hand of Ulster and underneath two hands clasped in friendship.

It

❦

The lovely blue Derry Express roared by at eight-twenty a.m., and I was always up by then. Or rather, always up on Monday for this was my favourite day of the week—the school week. Since we possessed no wireless, the parlour clock was adjusted by the times of passing trains, and usually the Derry. If the train ran a quarter-of-an-hour late, then accordingly we were late for school or church. But never on Mondays. Long before the great blue bird shook the house, my toast was made. It was clinic day.

First come, first served—if I could get to the clinic early and go through the treatment without waiting, I could be home again at eleven o'clock. The rest of the day was then free and my own. Not even the school inspector could force me to attend classes in the afternoon, for all school out-patients had a full day off.

On most Mondays I was among the first to run up the steps when the glass doors were unlocked. In the scrubbed, carbolic hall we presented cards with our number and then went into a large room, lined with benches on all four sides. A good consumptive green coloured its walls, and the ceiling matched the chalkiness of our faces, a not unsuitable decorative scheme for a tuberculosis clinic. Benches to the north were first attended to. Here we waited for a cross little man to weigh us and measure our heights. This done, we looked out for our friends and went to the east side. Rusty from the gang usually went with me, and as we lived in the same neighbourhood, we walked together to the building, and kept company throughout the treatment.

We most looked forward to meeting Harry. Willowy of limb, Harry was crowned with a head of luscious golden hair that got its strength from a bottle. But, alas, Harry had not much strength of his own, and between 'lie ins' at the sanatorium, brought his two small twin brothers to the Monday clinic. Harry was a walking card-index, and knew everybody's name, and details of case history. He suffered vicariously with us, our ills became as if they were his own, as though his condition was not in fact worse than ours. People said he had 'the gallopin' '.

'Have ya tried the new emulsion yet?' he would enquire with more than a mother's concern. 'Puts ya right off yer grub—it does—look at our Alec!' His fond look would then fall sadly on one of the spidery-limbed twins. A carefully manicured bejewelled hand would then straighten the brother's tie. 'Must look nice for Nursie.' And this niceness included himself for the hand then smoothed the worn but beautifully pressed flannel trousers, and for the fourth time put a comb through the glorious hair.

For his care over our welfare, Harry received our cruelty in return. We mimicked his reedy, effeminate voice and mocked at the movement of his willowy limbs. And on his birthday we took him a present. With profuse thanks, he meticulously unwrapped the parcel and found a peroxide bottle inside filled with water. As a first reaction he ruffled his hair to show us the natural gold of its roots. Then he went into a huff, and swept off the twins to the other end of the room. But we could see the tears well up in his large, pale blue eyes, and felt sorry, for it was not much of a visit without Harry there.

It

Being first, when we arrived the waiting-room was empty, but as the morning grew, it began to fill. Women came to sit, mummified in black shawls, that enveloped them like *burqas*. The wraps enhanced the fact that their bodies were dirty, and that the stench was beginning to overpower the earlier sharp carbolic smell. Their infected offspring played round them, wizened creatures, with old men's heads on children's bodies, thin and prematurely aged. Many of the children looked like this, including myself at one stage, and may have been the reason why people frequently mistook us as much older boys.

'There's wee Tony comin' in,' Harry would say as one of these dwarfs arrived with its shawled mother, 'It's his left,' meaning that tuberculosis had attacked the boy's left lung.

At last my turn with the nurses came round, and I hurried along antiseptic corridors to a room presided over by two dear old ladies in grocers' white coats, and with There's-a-fine-laddie voices. Temperature and pulse were measured and recorded, and file folders with sheets of red diagrams showing lungs and bodies were taken importantly down another corridor, while I returned to the hall again, this time to sit on the south side.

Perhaps the smell of oranges being peeled, and noisily sucked, now began to add flavour to the close atmosphere, bringing the cross little weighing man to open the windows. The draught sent the mums deeper into their shawls, like badgers viewing the world from their setts. Rumbles of disapproval broke into open objection to the air so callously admitted. And Harry, ever a champion of the down-trodden, spoke up sharply to the little man, 'If ya don't close it this instant, I'll go straight to Nurse'.

Smooth wheels of administration creaked occasionally when the doctors arrived late. The shawled figures, inanimate for the greater part, showed signs of restlessness. These women had walked long distances on foot, and had to go back the same way in order to be home by their hungry families' dinner-time. Blame for delays usually fell, quite unjustly, on the cross man, he being the nearest and most frequently seen, as he plied in and out on his weighing business. But all the mutterings and complaints in the world, would not have hurried affairs taking place beyond the white door.

'What are they fiddlin' with in there?—go and tell 'em Gert's in a hurry.'

But Gert must bide her time, even when the midday hooters filtered in from the shipyard and factory, and breaking point was reached.

'Here's me with me man's dinner in me hand', a woman would declare hotly, drawing a pink chain of sausages from the shawl's folds,—'and him home for one'.

To the doctors, their work must have seemed a fight with the odds against them. But they never stinted their efforts, and though the waiting queue hardly diminished, half an hour would be spent over one patient if necessary. This often happened to me, and in a darkened room amidst weird machinery attended both by a specialist and my regular doctor, I would lie on a mechanical sofa-table, while they prodded and sounded, tested and checked.

On the Mondays when an examination from the specialist was due, my mother came with me, and this meant a sacrifice for her. A morning's work was lost and with it, a fraction of the vital wages. But her patience never gave out, at last the doctors relaxed and told me I could jump up. Then the last wait began, for prescriptions for the free medicines and malt that helped in the struggle—the unending war against IT.

Neither the smells nor the waiting about could turn me from my love of Mondays. The clinic became almost a social club. But not so the dentist. Here, force was applied. Visits to

It

Frankenstein occurred two or three times a year, like it or not. The scene was laid in another clinic, as if prepared as a tableau from Hogarth. Parents and children huddled together in a small waiting-room, in an atmosphere emotionally charged by fear. When the terrifying ether began to creep out from the surgery, the children began to cry and scream, bringing everyone's nerves to a high pitch.

Then the door opened, an anonymous figure in a blue coat called out a name, and the child would be dragged, still screaming, into the cold room with the blinding lights. Another, bigger figure was waiting in another, bigger blue coat, and he plumped us into the chair. With arms held, and legs too if required, our mouths were forced open and a miniature dumb-bell inserted to keep jaws apart. Then gas. Through a universe unknown we sailed, while at the mundane level, probes or pincers struggled for victory. The yellow suns and red floods of unconsciousness mixed tentatively with the eye's normal sensations. 'Come to' we leaned in misery over a water-trough, while a shocked tongue explored the bloody cavities trying to discover how many teeth had gone.

But weekly visits to the clinic were only like baling out a leaky boat, eventually it must go into dry-dock. My 'lie in' at the hospital took a slice out of my life in most years. Until joining the gang, this was acceptable, giving me company and friends all day and every day. But when my soul belonged to Gandhi, such a long, enforced absence from the sally-bushes was irksome. For as long as possible I would conceal from my mother the fact that I was ill again.

Once, very late at night, when I felt terribly ill, I gave in and let her look at the abscesses on my body. She said little, but hurried me off to the baby-wear shop up the road. A member of the hospital committee owned it, and had a tall old-fashioned telephone that lived under a proportionately

It

long tea-cosy. Before ringing the hospital at that late hour, the woman insisted on seeing the seriousness of my condition. I was eleven, and resented having to drop my trousers.

Before midnight I lay soaking in a sulphur bath. And Big 'Ina was walking home to the other side of the city, to get in at least four hours' sleep, before starting her long day.

Bathed and nightshirted, I was led by a nurse into a darkened ward, lit like an aquarium by a green lamp on her table. She folded the bed-clothes in and crept away. Wondering at the renewed novelty of a strange bed and its crisp warm sheets, I became aware that the boy in the next bed also lay awake. It was Tiger. A protruding lower jaw, which clamped its teeth with unintentional ferocity over the upper row was responsible for the name.

' 'As she taken yer goods?' he whispered. His head jerked towards the nurse who had bathed me. She now sat, legs spread apart, in front of the gas fire by the screen, head dropped, hoping that fumes and sleep would make the night-duty hours pass more speedily. No, I replied to Tiger's question, I had not brought any food as the next day was visiting day. Big 'Ina had promised to send my elder sister with some things. Tiger's concern for my food derived from the fear that the nurse would help herself to it. Her great weakness, apparently, was digestive biscuits. The key to the cupboard where patients' own things were kept, lay on the table in a key-ring that she had only, in a moment of hunger, to reach out for. I resolved that anything brought for me on the morrow would be devoured at once or shared with Tiger.

And with that I fell asleep, to be awakened at once, it seemed, by daylight, and the nurse's anxious 'Are you swimming?' Recalling the usual practice, I readily showed her my dry bed. Not that my perfect control affected the hospital authorities in the least, I was obliged to have a rubber sheet—just in case. As daylight strengthened, a score of these mats were being mopped, the air heavy with urine as the unfortunates received long diatribes about being 'big boys'.

The incredibly brisk early morning routine was over, and we sat or lay clean-handed and shining-faced ready for the doctor. Perhaps for variety he would bring a group of students, like greyhounds being exercised. And while the great man made notes or asked questions, their inexperienced eyes would gaze down at my wretched body, an apparition, scarcely of flesh and blood at all.

Finding myself in hospital again was in the manner of a homecoming. I had known it all before, although in other wards round the corner. Before our dinner came in a trolley, everyone in the ward knew the details of my illness. By friendly nurses and chars, some of whom remembered me, I was able to send messages to other inmates. And in the lavatories, scalpel scars and other surgical signatures could be compared, often by prising the edge of a dressing. We loved to sit with the door bolted, so that when somebody else tried it we could cry out 'Who goes there—friend or enema?'

Being visiting day the *L'après midi d'un faune* after-dinner effect did not settle gently down, but a quiet excitement built up to three o'clock climax. All eyes watched the double doors and the dim hallway beyond, for familiar faces.

Cissy, of course, did not appear until visitors' hour was almost up, and even then, the treats from home were heavily plundered. That was one day at least when the night nurse was sure not to get much from me. Cissy, who had brought her friend, was in an independent, grown-up mood. She assumed control of the situation, said 'Who's this?' about Tiger, and seemed to approve of him. They cheered me up, and regaled me with tales about current love affairs. The details were probably exaggerated, but the general trend was true. Cissy and friend were both thirteen, but usually told their soldier or sailor pick-ups that they were seventeen. No visitors for

It

Tiger came that afternoon, and so when the love news had been imparted, Cissy turned to him and offered to read his hand.

Tiger's big day was Sunday. When the doors opened, his father was the first, without fail, to bolt up the polished centre aisle. A paper carrier-bag, held in a huge hand, fairly burst with good things. Tiger's mother was dead, his only visitor the father, whom I thought quite old. He worked as a caulker in the shipyard and thrilled us with stories of all the happenings there. Best among these were tales of bad-luck omens received before launchings. He lived for Tiger. When a lull came over the talk, he would sit, absurdly large on a small chair, looking proudly at the wasting figure lying in bed. His greeting never varied. The loaded paper bag was put down on the bed and with a face unable to take any more smile-stretching he asked, 'What have ya for yer ould da?' And he wept for joy to feel Tiger's fangs on his rough face.

But there were bitches who cast contemptuous glances at this marvellous father, declaring that he was permanently half-tight. True, the watery eyes and flowery Cyrano de Bergerac nose were suspect. Chief among his critics featured the evangelical Sister Winnie, who came to sing hymns on Sunday after the visitors had gone. Often she came early to talk with the dejected specimens whose whole visiting hour had been spent hoping against hope that someone they loved would appear in the door. When the visitors' leaving-bell rang desperately through the long corridors, and their last hopes vanished, Sister Winnie knew how to cheer and console. Her goodness was proverbial, and the penny she gave me for chocolate, after the slot-machine had swallowed my expanded make, was typical of her understanding for children.

Tiger would pull his father's sleeve and say excitedly 'Here's Sister Winnie.' As she passed, the man would beam at her and say kindly, 'Good-day to ya, Sister'.

It

Then Winnie's face would drain of its sweetness. To point the moral of salvation she replied haughtily, 'Don't you call *me* sister—I'm one of the Lord's.' It happened every Sunday.

Being 'saved' or not 'saved' divided the nurses. Most popular with the patients were the jolly 'unsaved' ones, who referred wickedly to their opposite numbers as the 'Gospel Belles'. Medical students and doctors preferred the sinners too. At Christmas we were for ever hopping out of bed to see the prettiest being waylaid under the mistletoe in the hall.

One of the nursing sisters wore a wig, and patients of many years' standing declared it had once been whisked off in a fight with another nurse, near the mistletoe. As Christmas approached, we hoped that the same thing would happen again—it would have made our Christmas. But that year we had to be content with a medical student grabbing a 'saved' nurse under the mistletoe. She struggled righteously and escaped by dealing him a heavy blow on the nose. Not without satisfaction we watched the blood spurt richly over his starched white jacket.

But these were high-lights, prominent events in a life led under the restraint of keeping in bed. More tedious hours we beguiled by making up rhymes about the nurses and their peculiarities, not forgetting their quarrels. We could go on for ever with lines like,

> *Cheer up Nurse McGinne, your name is everywhere*
> *You left Sister Brownwig crying in the chair,*
> *Crying for mercy, when mercy wasn't there,*
> *You got her on the trap, and swung her by the hair.*

I was practised at this sort of thing, as rhymes and rhythms in poetry had interested me from very early on. At home in an empty 'Black Magic' chocolate box with a red tassel, I kept my poetry clippings. We never took a daily newspaper regularly, but Old Clara next door had the 'Tele' (the *Belfast Telegraph*), and with her 'good' glasses on, perused the deaths column immediately the paper came. She read out the notices to her family, and if I was there I would listen specially to the verses of mourning. In a voice different from her normal one, tuned to a sentimental strain, she would recite,

> *For us she always done her best,*
> *May God grant her eternal rest.*

The following day, when Old Clara handed us the paper for various household and sanitary purposes, I cut the verses out, and the collection of snippets gradually filled the box. And while rambling in the city cemetery I culled poetry from the headstones and added it to the 'Black Magic' collection. I thought these jingles sad and beautiful.

The coming of Christmas compensated for all other dull moments in hospital, and we made its joys last from long before until long after normal celebrations outside the hospital. I feasted royally, on things never seen at home. Our family's seasonal fare consisted of a boiled hen, bought late on Christmas Eve from the market, when prices were at their lowest, the parish poor-box joint, and as a special treat a bottle of lime juice cordial, and apple tarts. No one knew exactly what would be included in the hospital Christmas dinner and tea, but our thoughts were distracted from this by entertainments given in the wards. And for two weeks every sect and schism of Protestant Belfast, and there seemed to be no end, came to sing carols for us. So hot on each other's heels were they, that sometimes one lot would hardly be out of the room before another was in, shuffling and arranging positions, while a portable harmonium was unfolded and set up.

Individuals appeared also, who were never seen at other times of the year. Men as well as women called on solitary

errands of mercy, to distribute little gifts. Our big cupboard
at the end of the ward became loaded with packets of dates
and arrowroot biscuits. A rumour sprang from nowhere
that a famous film star was coming to visit us. We collected
scraps of paper for autographs, about a dozen pieces each, so
that the star's handwriting could be given to friends at home.
Then, like a pricked bubble, the rumour collapsed, the actress
was not coming after all. Another rumour circulated, this
time that her visit had been prevented by the 'saved' nurses,
who had threatened to strike if any such ungodly person was
allowed in the building.

What a different attitude the 'unsaved' nurses adopted.
They would not have cared who came to see us, and asked
openly about our girl-friends and how we treated them. As
a reply, we either fabricated monstrous untruths, or left the
questions unanswered except for hints of behaviour so extravagant that we dare not divulge it.

The nurses encouraged us to write letters to our girls. Mine
of previous 'lie ins' had gone to Minnie Moore, who had a
mass of bright red ringlets and a face covered with freckles
like an avocet's egg. On the upper reaches of her thigh was
an autumn leaf, a birth-mark, and to be allowed a sight of
this was high privilege. For a time, Minnie had sat beside me
in school, and when I had eaten my lunch, I waited on her
doorstep to go back to school with her. In summer, for my
faithfulness she would give me a cool glass of sour buttermilk
with a pinch of baking-soda, and in winter a hot glass of
cabbage-water.

Billets-doux hummed along the wires of the internal com-
munication too, small, grubby notes carefully folded and
taken to their destination in a nurse's pockets. Only the sinners,
of course, could be asked to undertake such errands, and we
kept them busy running in and out of the girls' wards. On
rare occasions, one of the nurses would arrange for us to see

103

the object of our affection across the hall, and at Christmas, some of us actually met, flesh to flesh, under the mistletoe.

And also on request, the sinner-nurses would act as a marriage-bureau, answering our queries as to whether a nice girl about our own age could be found across the hall. The nurse would fold her hands together, the starched cuffs clicking, and pretend to think deeply. 'Doreen Smith with the lovely hair is rather lonely. Just your age. Suit you?' We said she would, and off went the first letter. Then came the exciting period of waiting for the answer, and perhaps a glimpse across the hall.

A sense of urgency often accompanied these wild love-letters, for the girls' ward seemed to have many more deaths than our own. It had been known for some notes never to get an answer, or for a regular correspondence to cease suddenly. We viewed the situation without a trace of emotion, and every morning enquired eagerly after the latest departure, as if it were no more than a train leaving a station. Sentimental reactions were the proper realm of grown-ups. The 'saved' staff regarded death as their province and gave us the news. If death impended, they liked to be around, even when off-duty, so that the little heart could be pointed heavenward. 'Sadie from the far ward has gone,' we would be informed. 'She sang a hymn that very afternoon, so she did, and had a glorious wee passing'. And for the rest of the day a watch would be kept at the windows to see Sadie's coffin depart.

My visitors on open days never included the great-aunts. The bowels of their compassion were definitely shut up against me, for news of my doings with the gang and of police interviews had reached their sacred ears. They made no pretence about their thoughts on my condition. It was a proof to them of a just, eye-for-eye exacting God. They had told me in their sharp way that I had inherited all sorts of diseases from my 'white-livered da'.

It

But their God forsook them.

'If you go on like this for two weeks more' said the doctor, 'we'll think about packing you off home.'

Until these words, measurable time had ceased, the sand in the hour-glass had stuck in the narrow neck. But now the blockage was released, the grains began to flow again. Those two weeks stretched interminably ahead, longer than the past three months had been, longer than my whole life. All I wanted was the last visitor bringing my clothes, so that I could fling off the hideous grey garment, one of the night-shirts that made us all look like girls. We hated the nightshirts and the milk puddings, and dreamed so often about the civil-ized life that waited outside. It was a life that seemed, in retro-spect, so unbelievably rich with its smells from Billy's fish-and-chip shop and the screaming wonders of the Saturday penny cinema, visions that sometimes rose up and devoured our whole thinking.

The promised oasis in the desert of weeks proved not to be a mirage. On the appointed morning the doctor stood at the bedside, making the momentous decision. The world stood still, as he looked at charts, whispered to the ward-sister, muttered to himself, twisted his mouth and pursed his lips with 'H'm' and 'Ah', and took quick glances at my tense, expectant face. He cleared his throat. I knew then the decision was made, but which way?

'Well, my boy, you can leave on Friday.'

Friday—wonderful Friday—forty-eight hours away! Al-most before the doctor had gone I seized a pencil and paper and multiplied the hours by sixty, and the minutes by sixty again to get the seconds. I wrote the score down and then began to cross it off. After being asked ten times in an hour for the exact time, the nurses' patience frayed, and they ans-wered my question, 'Time to go to sleep'. And the boy in the end bed by the door could not always hop out to see the hall clock for me. It would never come, those thousands of minutes would never be crossed out.

But the dawn, as all dawns that ever were, broke and it was Friday, and I was having my departing bath, my ears poked and toenails cut. My samples were checked, and the last crumbs in the cupboard divided out. Tiger, growing weaker every day, could not sit up in bed. With wide eyes he watched Cissy arrive with my jersey and pants. The whole ward, and the next one, and all the girls' wards on the other side were talking about the same thing—I was going out, and on my own two feet, shaky though they were.

Dumbfounded and envious, all eyes were at the window as I went by the flower-beds in the garden. All except Tiger's.

To show them how free and strong I was, I tried a somersault in the grass, looking up again to throw a dozen kisses. Then Cissy and I were through the iron gates where Gandhi and others from the gang had tried abortively to get through on visiting days. Because they had no yellow card, the gate-keeper had turned them away. Now of course, yellow cards did not matter any more. I looked for a piece of coal, so that I could spit on it, and throw it over my left shoulder, and swear never to go back to hospital again.

Cissy, meanwhile, was trying to interest me in a call at the sweet-shop, instead of using the two halfpennies on the tram home—my end-of-hospital treat.

Of course, there was no argument, only thoughts of gob-stoppers or a make's worth of dulce. The old life had begun again.

The Sands of Down

Away went that train down to Bangor West, County Down, the loveliest, fastest train ever, for I was going off on my very first holiday. It seemed as if slow, agonizing years passed from the time when we initially heard about it, until the actual day arrived. Holiday, the word of magic! But anything could go wrong; even at the last minute, some twist of fate could snatch away the holiday. But nothing did. My mother and sisters and I scrambled out of the train, and made our way to the summer home for poor people, trailing our luggage which was parcels of brown paper and newspaper.

We had to share a room with two other families; a young widow like my mother and her son, and an elderly woman and her granddaughter. The old woman never failed to amaze me, when every night and morning she struggled in or out of her combinations, standing on thin legs like a stork at the edge of a pool. The other boy had some pet mice, and one night he let them run across the room, as the spindly apparition struggled out of its woollens in the semi-darkness. Poor old girl, she thought the mice were in her coms, in the bed, and she shrieked so much that an attendant came and moved her, granddaughter and all, to another room.

Our relatives in Canada, so my mother reckoned, would be pleased to have photographs of the holiday, and accordingly she borrowed a box camera for the snaps. We 'borrowed' a

The Sands of Down

raft from the yachting club up the beach, and my sisters, the boy from our room and I, sat on it, while my mother tried her hand at the complications of a camera. It was a novelty, and as she was finding out how to work it, a strong current took hold of the raft. The tide was going out, and within minutes we were swept far beyond reach. Luckily for us, the boating club people, who had probably disapproved of their raft being taken, saw the danger and rescued us in a motor-boat, thereby adding another thrill to our day.

We enjoyed food which to us was marvellous, though in reality it was nothing more than of the plain and wholesome variety. But we did not have to scrape pennies together for it and then wonder where the next was coming from; for every meal-time the tables were mysteriously loaded. In return for this miracle of loaves, attendance at a morning session of Bible reading was necessary. In the evenings we had to attend various forms of the evangelical whirlpool, which sought to suck us all into its vortex; there were plenty of opportunities of 'coming forward' to be 'saved'. Not that we minded, for every day we learnt a new chorus until our heads were crammed to capacity. We knew everything from 'Climb, climb up sunshine mountains' to,

> *Down to the flames I'll never go*
> *That's where the devil reigns below,*
> *So I'll keep my promise bright*
> *And shout with all my might,*
> *But down to the flames I'll never go.*

On most afternoons, weather permitting, we bundled off to Bangor proper. Here were sandy beaches to play on, clean and left in ridges by a receding tide, waiting naked like an artist's canvas. But even here we could not play as we liked, could not cover that canvas with our own inventions of sand castles and moats. Yet another evangelical movement waited for us. Bribing us with prizes, it cajoled us into making wide circles of sand pies. In the centre of these, scriptural texts must be written, and the whole decorated with rich ornaments of shells and various seaweeds. Like a rash of ringworm the Bangor sands bore these circular sermons for long stretches. As if a pre-historical race was building defensive forts, young souls laboured to beautify the many versions of 'God is Love', 'Jesus Saves' or 'Trust in the Lord'. All the skill and ingenuity was lavished on them that bakers devote to sugar icing on birthday cakes. Whether we lacked faith or art nobody could guess, but certainly no prizes for such righteous work, on which we spent many hours, ever came my family's way.

On the Saturday when we took our farewells to the Bangor sands and the gaunt old house, dozens of bunches with mixed flowers were put on the side-tables in the dining-room. After breakfast and final prayers and doxologies and all the rest of it, the matron stood at the door. Her good-byes to the outgoing crowd were given with handshakes and flowers for each of us.

My mother saw a bunch composed nearly all of sweet-peas, her favourite flower. Waiting her chance, she held back until the matron picked it up, and then pressed forward. Luck was out, for another woman pushed in front and got the heavenly scented blooms. Smiling broadly, the matron gave us a very gay bunch. But my mother, disappointed over the other, buried her nose in it, pulled a wry face and declared the kitchen cat had been busy in the bunch. And as we hurried along to the station, not knowing whether we were happy or sad, the whole family's jealous hate was turned on the woman who had got the sweet-peas—*our* sweet-peas.

After that first year my mother could not afford to take time off work to go again. I was sent to a holiday home attached to an orphanage on the yellow sands farther along the County Down coast. My sisters went to a similar home for poor girls elsewhere.

Without the rest of my family, holidays did not look so attractive, and the sunshine of afternoons splashing in the blue water I dreamt about, was clouded by home-sickness. At this first separation I was only eight, and realized how big and empty the world can be. Besides this, I had gone with older boys, who mocked at what they called my 'swanky' voice; for, not that anyone ever knew why, I never spoke with much of an Irish brogue.

These boys boasted that they came from the very worst and wildest of Belfast's grimmest slums. I could hardly understand what some of them said. But I knew they must regard me as from a different layer of society altogether, and laughed me to scorn on that account.

The bus journey was interminable, the ragging unending. When the bus finally turned in to the home, I bolted for the lavatory with my parcel. Secure at last, I sat down to have a good weep. Somebody else came in and tried my door, and finding it locked went into the next cubicle. The seat squeaked as he sat down and began to talk through the wall. He sounded much older than me, and I was afraid to answer for dread that he, like all the others, would mock my accent.

I froze when I heard a scuffling, and my neighbour's head appeared over the partition. Fierce eyes stared down as I jumped off the seat trying to pull up my trousers. The eyes belonged to Jimmy Price.

He demanded to know from what street in Belfast I hailed and when informed, asked if I knew Granny Bell in number ninety-eight. Of course I knew Granny Bell with her ancient Edwardian boots buttoned up the sides as though for skating, and her distended nostrils black from the constant stuffing in of snuff. Her heart was of gold, and she would always give a child a make who ran an errand for her. The youngest ones were afraid of her horse-like appearance, which blood-shot eyes sometimes enhanced. Jimmy was delighted that I knew all about her, and said proudly that she was his real grandma, though she was universally known as Granny Bell.

After this encounter in the lavatory, I was secure under Jimmy's protection. There was no doubting that the young pig grunted like the old sow, for Jimmy had his grandmother's kind heart—especially towards me.

Later, on our first evening, we all had to form a double queue in the dining-room, brother with brother, or friend with friend, to arrange the sharing of beds. I soon realized how lucky I was when Jimmy chose me as bed partner. No one dared now to call me a jinny because of my voice, and the boy disinfectant-orderly dared not throw off our sheets in the morning before we were awake, to spray the narrow bed with Flit.

Now that I have travelled and seen how respectable the world has become, the days of my childhood seem particularly wild; but nothing compared with Jimmy Price's. Even for me he was better than Tarzan, or the most daring gang-leader of our Belfast slums. A hundred boys held him as hero and looked to him for leadership. No wonder; his was the spiciest slang, and his methods the best for raiding orchards or gas-meters, and getting into the cinema for nothing. He had enormous feet, the shoes for these being nearly twice the normal size for his age, but this only added to his prowess.

Apart from giant feet, and impressive locks of oily black hair which kept their superb waves by butter-mixture stolen from the kitchen, nature had been generous to Jimmy in most ways. His privileged friends were allowed to try on the great shoes, and see how really vast they were. We all stole admiring glances at a long scar studded with stitch marks, said to be the result of a knife-fight. No row of medals could have impressed us younger boys more.

The Sands of Down

To be Jimmy's special friend made me very proud, and when my turn came as table-orderly, I always sorted out the heels of bread-and-mix for him to eat secretly after lights-out.

For me, life at the holiday home was one continuous delight, especially as Jimmy shielded me from older boys' teasings. I shall never forget the smell of buddleia which lay heavily on the air in the overhanging driveway; or the vastness of the cow parsley like a miniature forest which we crept through to rob my first orchard; or the chilling dampness of the old tunnel under the main road, which we used for getting down to the beach.

On Sunday there was always red and green jelly and semolina pudding for tea, and the inevitable hot session of evangelical choruses every night before bed-time. Easily the most popular of these was,

> *Get them out, get them gone,*
> *All the little rabbits in the fields of corn,*
> *Envy, jealousy, hatred and pride,*
> *All the lurking sins that in my heart abide.*

Perhaps we liked this one and its rousing tune most, because we had our own version, sung secretly in the dormitory or the porcelain retreat of the lavatories.

> *Get them in, get them in,*
> *All the lovely wingies from the Button B tin,*
> *Gub-stops, ice-cream, the whole bally lot,*
> *For me ould rubber belly's as big as your pot.*

A 'wingie' was our affectionate term for wing which meant a penny, and a halfpenny was a make. The Button B tin was the telephone kiosk money box, and so the whole chorus referred to our skill in getting pennies out of the machine, and the good things they could be spent on. Looking back now, it is surprising how many pennies were got out, simply by pressing Button B; and of course, we made it a matter of strict principle never to pass a kiosk without doing so.

What a comical collection we must have looked on the beach! None of us had costumes and the home did not provide proper swimming trunks, but old-fashioned ones with legs and tops. But even these were discarded from the permanent orphanage, and were in a sad condition, minus limbs or vital straps, even the remaining pieces being full of magnified moth-holes. Without discrimination as to size, they were handed out, wholeness being the criterion. So, armed with these, down to the beach we ran, where some of the smallest boys climbed into long ragged garments reaching to the ankle, while someone like Jimmy had a good piece of bottom escaping like a red balloon.

Clad in these strange sea-garments, we passed happy days, and clambered for hours over the rocks, collecting the dulce seaweed to dry and take home for our families, or jumping on the bladderwrack to make the gas vesicles go pop. Then we would look for the shining sugar laminaria with its crumpled, frilly edge to save up as a barometer. And when it hung, dank and soft, on the wall at home, it would serve not only to warn of threatening rain, but to remind us of the sea-shore search and the rock-scrambling. Some of this seaweed we found clinging tenaciously to stones, and these we threw high into the air, and watched them falling to earth again, followed by the fluttering kite-like trail of seaweed. And among the rocks also we took our string and bent pins and went fishing, or feeling more energetic, attacked each other with the sword blades of the razor-shells.

Our adventures were strictly inshore affairs for we were not allowed to try our luck among the breakers and currents farther out. The strongest amongst us occasionally waded or swam beyond the safety line, and then a whistle would shrill from the beach where the supervisor sat, and punishment would be visited on the whole group.

Such a teeming life lurked or squiggled, swam or floated in the still mirror-pools amongst the rocks, that I never felt much urge to venture into the sea itself. Looking for the strange friendly creatures that eked out their secret little lives between the rushing in of one tide and the next, could so absorb my interest that rolling seas, only a few yards distant, ceased to exist.

And where no pools could be found, along the beach I searched for weird pebbles, or glass ground by the threshing to and fro of many tides, always hoping to catch the sparkle of a diamond. But when the sun glared like brass and not a whisper of wind brushed among the sea-grasses, then I would confront the sea where it lay, horizon melted all away. And on the metal-smooth surface, I would skate and bounce flat, oval pebbles until the supply was exhausted, or someone called with another distraction.

At other times, when the tang of salt and seaweed seemed stronger in the breeze, and the sea's perspective ended in a sharp indigo line, Scotland could be seen. What a subject for boasting when I got home to Belfast again—I had seen the coast of Scotland! My experience would colour me in my friends' eyes as a well-travelled man. The thin grey ribbon of not-too-substantial land, although only just visible, was beyond all doubt another country. Nobody could argue with me now about having seen a strange land. Bonnie Scotland it was, where all the real kilties lived, with its lochs of live monsters, and hills where the men gathered white heather to bring to Belfast for the Cup Final.

Life was not all play. We had our share of work too, and a system of orderlies looked after this. Outside, digging and weeding had to be done, and domestic chores such as polishing

The Sands of Down

floors and laying the tables, setting out stacks of bread with mix.

One year the lot of disinfectant-orderly fell to me, shared with a boy called Pink, a shortened Pinkerton. Our less pleasant duties included the cleaning out of drains by hand, though one day I was overjoyed to find a penny in a handful of mud.

Pink immediately claimed half of my find as his due, although he had been farther along at the next gully. Jimmy, who was on the potato-peeling squad, objected to his demand. Pink called to his brother, who in spite of his nickname Parsnip was a match for Jimmy. Over went the buckets of peelings, the fresh white potatoes went flying, black eyes were shared all round, and I got a long knife wound on the left arm that I used as a battle trophy for years after.

Boys from the various Belfast districts clung loyally together, and all joined in if one of their number was attacked by someone outside the group. We egged each other on by singing,

> The Shankill Road's a dirty ould 'ole
> Sandy Row's the dandy

according to ours and the opponents' address.

The fights were common to all, and so were the punishments meted out after such outbreaks. Nuisance more than pain attached to the punishments, and the worst sentence was to have a ban put on going down to the beach, the learning of scripture in the play-room being substituted instead. Under such duress I learnt by heart chapter fifty-three of Isaiah, the thirty-second Psalm and every single verse from the *aleph* to the *caph* of the hundred-and-nineteenth Psalm. Only the war and evacuation from Belfast doubtless saved me from ploughing my way to *tau*.

The mystery of language, the strings of meaningless symbols in the Psalms, especially the thirty-second, were a source of immense satisfaction and we never grew tired of wondering what on earth, or out of it, was intended by, 'When I kept silence, my bones waxed old through my roaring all the day long. For day and night thy hand was heavy upon me; my moisture is turned into the drought of summer. Selah.' That was one we could not completely fathom, though we had our own interpretations for most other things, and the recurrent ailments of the psalmist's bladder.

We also had some smart questions ready for the large, purple-faced preacher who came to talk to us on Sunday night. After the service he had a question-time and every year there was bound to be a wag who asked 'If Eve was the first woman, who did her childer marry, Mister?' Our satisfaction lay in hearing the question; the answer, if any, was unimportant.

The whole subject of sex was taboo, and the solid, evangelical housewives winced at our language. They quickly set us more scripture to learn when they heard us swear. When we made walking excursions to the different towns, we chalked enormous phallic signs on the sea-front wall which the pious eyes could not possibly miss.

So bad did they consider us that girls from the permanent orphanage were kept strictly behind the strong wire fence that separated us. On the beach we were also banned from talking to strangers, or indeed anyone but the rosy-cheeked matrons.

But it would have taken more than wire fences to keep us from having mild affairs with the girls, for like all forbidden fruit it seemed sweetest. We could always wink and mouth kisses, and sometimes put out hands to touch them, when their crocodile passed ours on the road or the shady avenue. The scribbling of notes to pass through the wire was another secret source of contact.

The Sands of Down

Virtuous isolation of the girls was necessary to ensure this safety from the animals of the slum jungle. They had, after all, been rescued from it by the good evangelicals, and stood some chance of one day making worthy citizens, obedient, loyal, and 'saved'. But well the matrons knew what little chance they had of converting the sordid beasts of the summer holiday homes. All they could hope for was that the 'WORD' might fall into some crevice amongst the stony places of our minds. Meanwhile we must pace up and down the fence, like zoo lions, sniffing a distant bit of skirt, or pay the penalty of more direct intercourse—the learning of Psalms.

But long ago, in the streets at home, we had thrashed out the complete process of reproduction, and by now were on familiar terms with it. We used our talk about it simply because we knew, for unimaginable reasons, that grown-ups became embarrassed whenever sex was mentioned. In our own house, we were forbidden to raise the topic even though grass-widows, 'big diddies', hairy chests, and the forms of Mae West, entwined themselves in ordinary conversation. When tempers frayed, then coarse words making references to fornication or sexual organs were freely bandied and reverberated in no uncertain manner between the walls overloaded with sacred writings. Still, we might not raise the serpent's head in the normal course of speaking.

My first year at school had taught me something of the more sophisticated aspects of human behaviour. A small boy proudly inflated his prize balloon, up and up it went growing to generous proportions, fat and long. The older children who gathered round then began to laugh at something I failed to understand. Into the middle of the merriment a teacher stepped. Her lips compressed, and her eyes went hard and black. With a single blow she burst the balloon and with another sent the astonished child into floods of tears. She draped the piece of white rubber over the end of her cane like a dead snake, gripped the boy, and the procession went off to the headmaster for further punishment. An afternoon of oppression ensued, and teachers conferred in whispers. I had seen my first contraceptive.

Naturally enough, we sought out those passages in the Bible which obscurely refer to the human body and its functions—but why were they included in the ban? Some of our elders were prim enough to insist that 'belly' must always be 'stomach' or even 'tummy', even if the scriptures pleased to use such a word.

It really puzzled me to know why some words in the 'Grand Old Book' were swear-words; could they be, as they were in the Bible? After all the 3,566,480 letters, 810,697 words, 31,175 verses, 1,189 chapters and 66 books of holy scripture, were most sacred, so grown-ups said in one breath; and in the next reprimanded us for using some of its words, in spite of the precepts of the chorus,

> *Every letter in the Book is mine,*
> *Every chapter, every verse, every line,*
> *All are messages of love divine,*
> *Every letter in the Book is mine.*

All sexual activities were lumped together under the general epithet 'dirty tricks'. We were left to find out for ourselves the changes taking place in our bodies at this time, changes which weak lungs and thin bodies did nothing to mute, but rather accelerated. Undoubtedly no teacher, clergyman or parent would stoop so low as to discuss 'dirty tricks'. In spite of all the mumbo-jumbo, the smoke screen of respectability thrown around what was clearly a big factor in life, we waxed very knowledgeable on most forms of sexual behaviour, long before we were able to practise them.

Homosexuals also entered our experience. Apart from Harry at the clinic, whom we could not quite make out except that he was a big jinny and very popular, there was a man called Moses Greer. He minced and flapped his wrists; he swaggered his hips; laughed and talked in a cracked, high voice; and loved to be whistled at by the corner-boys. He used to chat with the women about going to dances, and the dresses he would wear.

Nobody minded Mosie in the least, and most were sorry when he was sent to jail for a robbery at the old dame's shop whose dustbin had provided me with burnt honeycomb. I often thought of poor Mosie and wondered if he would be allowed his pale lemon ball-dress in the prison. Local opinion said that he had only stolen to get money in order to buy Sandy, his soldier friend, out of the army.

Although sensitive about things of the flesh, the female guardians of the holiday home were extremely good women, very efficient and generally concerned about our young and lusty souls. The rigid righteousness of our surroundings irked at times, but we enjoyed the holidays immensely, living through the long winter with many a thought of next summer by the sea.

The last holiday before my evacuation from Belfast proved a lonely one, for Jimmy Price was not there. I heard he was in trouble with the police and had been sent to an approved school. I missed him and the soul seemed gone out of the home we had shared for five summers. The sands that year bore no imprint of the large shoes, nor of the army boots he was obliged to wear in latter years. What crusts there were when I was table-orderly, I could keep for myself.

But I did not desert Jimmy. When back in Belfast after the holiday, I saw the crocodile of approved-school boys going to church. I rushed up to Jimmy, who was as cheerful as ever, to hear his news.

The Boys of Sandy Row

❦

'No Pope here', 'Not an inch', 'God save the King', and 'Remember 1690' were signs we saw every day. They appeared in huge permanently painted letters on the gable ends of the streets round about. Although our street lay midway between Falls Road, the centre of everything Catholic in Belfast, and Sandy Row, the strongest Orange quarter, we were staunchly Protestant. Even ruder slogans against His Holiness decorated some gables; together with elaborate paintings, some twenty feet or more high, of coronation scenes complete with flowering robes, regalia, and recognizable portraits of King George V and Queen Mary. The crossing of Boyne Water by King Billy, with flying banners and flashing swords, was, however, the favourite topic for these vast outdoor murals.

We had a mural too in the backyard of our house, but only a painted crown on the whitewash under the window-sill. Higher up, only just visible, remained the fragments of King Billy's charger, the open Bible, a lurid eye through the clouds, Jacob's ladder, the rainbow, and Noah's ark, painted years before by my father while in a mood of patriotism. Whatever they represented religiously and politically, the pictures added a dash of colour and life to the drab mien of the streets.

We tried to reckon how much an ordinary Mickey would have to pay at confession for a week's sins. It was our firm belief that every sin had to be paid for in hard cash, and that was why so many Catholics were publicans—unlike so many others their tills were always full of cash.

For one particular crime we could never forgive the Mickeys; their hatred of the Bible. All Catholics were under orders, we were told, to burn any scripture they found, especially New Testaments. The old song supported us,

> *The intriguing Paypishes surround this loyal and ancient town*
> *They tried you know not long ago to pull the Bible down*
> *And to destroy it root and branch they often have combined*
> *But from Sandy Row we made them fly like chaff before the wind.*

What pride we enjoyed for living so near to Sandy Row—the Boys of Sandy Row, stalwarts of our Orange Order.

We imagined also that newly dead popes were embalmed like Takabuti in the museum, and then put on display as human money-boxes; and that when they were stuffed so full that not another penny would go in, they were canonized and became saints.

Takabuti, the Egyptian mummy, a house-mistress of a priest of Amunre, reclined in a case at the museum not altogether without a vestige of former dignity. She could never have imagined, three thousand years before, the tiny faces that would press so often against the glass of her exhibition table. Her hair and teeth, whole though shrivelled and discoloured, and her delicate foot complete with flesh and toenails, attracted as much attention as perhaps they had so long ago. Certainly the priest of Amunre could not have paid her more attention than we did. However, much as we loved Takabuti and her wimple of blue beads, other kinds of priests occupied our minds—those of Rome.

Crowding out any other aspects of history, our schools dinned into us over and over again the Protestant story. On leaving school, and that none too early for my liking, I had no notion of the world's past other than a few prehistoric tales and dreary details concerning our Protestant faith and the unrelieved darkness of Rome. The particular rack on which they tortured us appeared in the form of a small, buff covered booklet entitled *How we differ from Rome*.

With what surprising, singeing pains my hands and fingers often smarted when a cane or strap was administered because on being asked 'How does Pope Honorius, writing in 1221, refer to the entry of the English into Ireland?' I could not furnish the correct answer. 'Pope Honorius states that "the English entered Ireland by the authority of the Apostolic See and made it obedient to the Church of Rome".' Really! No excuse could be offered, they told me so frequently, probably every day, certainly every week; I had no reason, on being asked to 'Quote from Pope Adrian's letter to Henry II', for failing to report that 'Pope Adrian states :- "While as a Catholic prince you intend to widen the bounds of the Church we are anxious to introduce a faithful plantation in that land" (of Ireland).' The complete horrid booklet had to be learnt by heart, before we could be upgraded to commit the Prayer Book catechism to memory, and finally present ourselves, suitably primed, for confirmation.

This picture appears black, but a lighter side did exist, a comic-relief provided by intimate details of the popes' private lives. Before we tumbled out of our cradles, we knew of the unspeakable behaviour by the pontiffs and their courts. The goings-on of the Borgias were as familiar as the affairs of the next-door neighbour.

Even proper history books, we were assured, disclosed the antics at the papal court, with Roman strumpets running round and burning their bare bottoms on the great lighted candles of the Vatican. Nuns undergoing initiation were sometimes forced to play the part of these naked shepherd-esses—until too old for orgies. Then they were given the

The Boys of Sandy Row

flowing habits to cover up the singe marks on their buttocks and legs, and sent back to Ireland or wherever they came from. No wonder our preachers referred in horror to Rome as the Scarlet Woman! And little wonder amongst our first nursery rhymes was,

> *If I had a penny*
> *Do you know what I would do?*
> *I would buy a rope*
> *And hang the pope*
> *And let King Billy through.*

After all, our unswerving loyalty to the British crown was through King Billy—William of Orange, the man who defeated the Catholic Stuarts, the Irish and French, in the famous battle at the Boyne river.

From these allegiances the greatest spectacular event of the Ulster year took place on the twelfth of July. How wise of William to win his battle at the height of summer, so that festivities in its honour through the centuries after could be held in sunshine and fine weather! How we children waited for that day, and for the day preceding, when the riot of decorations received finishing touches in the streets. A Union Jack hung from every house, and masses of bunting crisscrossed the street from upper windows; crowns and mystical triangles; crescent moons each with seven stars, and flaming suns with faces; the burning bush and David's sling and five stones; streamers; red, white and blue rosettes bloomed in a profuse garden of paper and linen.

Each street vied with the next in the splendour of the main piece, its triumphal arch. Spanning between two houses, bedizened with orange and purple streamers, the arch was studded with pictures of British royalty. The climax of these preliminaries to the Twelfth was the lighting of bonfires. In the manner of the English November Fifth, we had effigies

The Boys of Sandy Row

of Catholic leaders, that had sat for weeks on street corners collecting pennies, and which were solemnly consigned to the flames like Guy Fawkes.

Before the ashes had lost their red hearts, the drums of Lambeg rolled like thunder through the summer night and ushered in our Glorious Twelfth. Day dawned; everyone was up early, ready to go out and see the sights and watch the traditional 'walk to the field'. It was a public holiday, as important to us as the Fourth of July in the U.S.A.

For miles along the Lisburn Road, thousands waited to see the Orangemen walk in procession behind elaborate banners painted with symbols of their secret society. To us Belfast boys, the Black men we looked for in the procession were not negroes, but the most respected holders of the highest rank within the hierarchy of the Order. Purple men followed them in precedence and lastly the ordinary Orangemen, all three wearing sashes coloured after their rank and bordered with a heavy gold fringe.

Everywhere orange colour flamed in sash and banner, and in the lily which people wore. They twined in bunches with sweet-williams on top of the standards, for the orange-lily was as sacred to us as the shamrock was to the Mickeys or Fenians.

> Do you think that I would let
> A dirty Fenian cat
> Destroy the leaf of a lily-o,
> For there's not a flower in Ireland,
> Like King Billy's orange-lily-o.

Such sights! Such music, churning the Protestant blood in our veins! For my first eight Twelfths I had needs be content with trailing through the crowds, craning for a glimpse of glory, straining to see the cymbals' flashing as zing-zing-zing they crashed in a flash of sun, pushing my way through

The Boys of Sandy Row

a forest of arms and legs to catch the dozens of pipe-bands, the flutists, and the drummers. The drummers came between each Lodge, flaying the hides of the big bass drums from Lambeg, where, naturally, they made the finest drums in the world. The huge cylinders were painted and decorated in gold, red, and orange with figures and patterns, crests and royal coats-of-arms in a whirligig of colour and line. It was considered a point of honour by some Lambeggers to beat the great drums so hard, and for so long, that wrists chafed the drum's edge until the skin became sore or even until cuts and bleeding resulted.

As expression of loyalty to a Protestant throne it would have been hard to find anything finer. But as music the effect was open to question. Whether of pipes or flutes or brass, or simply four of the gigantic Lambeg drums, each band felt that responsibility for the day's music rested solely, and by no means lightly, on their shoulders. Consequently they blew, blasted, and banged as heartily as wind and muscle knew how. For a single band in isolation this would have been admirable, but since one band succeeded another long before the first one was out of earshot, closely followed by yet more, and all playing different music, the total effect was overwhelming.

Unsurpassable day! In the pomp's midst, we tried to see friends from our neighbourhood's Lodges, and waited especially for Nodding Will to come. He lived two doors away from us, was old and had a twitching, shell-shocked head. But he was also a Black man and because of this rode in state in an open landau, clad in his best dickie and Sunday bowler.

The very first time my mother allowed me to follow the Orange procession to Finaghy Field, where the brave followers of King Billy met, I lost myself. Holiday mood had seized everyone, money went like water, and so many lemonades and iced cakes were given to the lost boy that he was ill. But not so ill that he could not hear his name called over the loudspeakers, a thrill with an exquisite edge, the climax of climaxes, the gilding indeed of the orange-lily. The Field was Elysian for me on that first day, for I went round collecting hundreds of coloured bottle-tops, which I fastened to my jersey, so that by the time I arrived home, exhausted with excitement, I was as scaly as a crocodile.

But Orange celebrations did not occur only on the Twelfth, for later in the year children sat out on the backyard walls, singing Orange ballads as the trains went by crammed with Black men going to the traditional closing of the gates of Derry. Although we enjoyed these celebrations as much as the grown-ups, we knew that serious feelings underlay the festivities. We had odd ideas on many things, but not about the reasons for these demonstrations.

In school nobody ever told us about Marie Antoinette or Marshal Foch, but we knew Louis XIV and Robert Lundy the treacherous governor of Derry. We might not know the date of the French Revolution but we did know that in 1688, thirteen young men, apprentices in the city, closed the gates of Derry in the face of the Catholic soldiers. We would forget our avoirdupois tables, but we remembered well enough that during the famous siege a dog's head cost two-and-sixpence, a rat or a quart of horse blood one shilling, and a handful of chickweed one penny. Dogs were fattened on the dead, and sold for five-and-sixpence per quarter carcass. Our greatest bed-time story was of the fat gentleman who hid himself for three days because several of the garrison troops had looked on him with greedy eyes. It was our heritage, and we were proud of it.

Confident of the city's surrender, James II himself went outside the walls of Derry to receive it. Instead, the beleaguered Protestants lined the walls and shouted 'No Surrender', which we fancied still resounded in our own breast as we watched the Black men go off to the famous scene. On the gable walls, along with the murals of coronations and anti-papal slogans, 'No Surrender' was also painted. When we drank our lemonade we toasted,

> *To the goose that grew the feather,*
> *To the hand that wrote No Surrender.*

The passing of the years, which swept the heroic 17th century further and further away, also brought nearer the time when I could graduate from being a thrilled bystander to an actual member of the Orange Order. I joined a junior Lodge, a proud day indeed for it was the 'Loyal Sons of William', whose headquarters were in Sandy Row itself. To be reckoned amongst the Boys of Sandy Row who had made the Mickeys go 'like chaff before the wind', was high honour and laid grave claims on my own courage. And now I would most certainly get a good place in heaven and be able to see King Billy and the Protestant martyrs. Our Bible spoke of four-and-twenty elders before the great white throne, and we deduced that this meant King Billy and company, to whom also were given the key to the bottomless pit where the Mickeys would go.

At my Lodge enrolment ceremony I had to stand outside the sacred locked doors of the inner chamber, trembling and waiting in a gloomy passage. Then before the whole assembly wearing its glittering regalia my name was put forward and approved. The doors opened and my sponsors emerged to lead me in, keeping position on both sides of me. I was marched through the columns of Loyal Sons. I was now shaking physically and almost incoherent as I swore to keep the Lodge password.

A concert took place afterwards, and I won first prize for declaiming the tale of the boy who stood on the burning deck. The Lodge wanted threepence for enlisting me, and I had only a penny. A bad beginning, to fall into arrears, but nevertheless I left the hall with an impressive penknife loaded with unusual blades and gadgets which must have cost at least two-and-sixpence. Such a possession had no appeal for me, and I gave it to Gandhi in exchange for a tin of condensed milk.

Such a careless attitude could not be adopted towards the secret password. This frightened me very much, for I reputedly talked in my sleep. And my fear of divulging the special word was not because of loyalty to the Lodge, but rather fear that my sisters, or people in the hospital when I went in, would hear it, and tell it to their friends. And eventually Catholic ears would hear it and this would bring catastrophe on us, and we would be hounded from Belfast for breaking so solemn a vow. The Order's shadow fell everywhere in the city, and I kept the wretched word and felt separated from my family by the Lodge.

When I got home from my enrolment, little Helen wanted to know everything that happened, especially if I had had to ride the goat. Until then we had been as thick as inkleweavers. But now the hocus-pocus of secret societies inserted a wedge between us. Big 'Ina overheard us and gave me a meaning look to keep silence, and I knew the Lodge doings must burn unrelieved in my breast, and Helen be content with a slap for presuming to enquire into such things.

Junior Lodges had their big parade on a different day from the elders, normally on Easter Tuesday; and we made an excursion by train, assembling again at the other end. Nothing could quieten us as we waited at the station, milling chaotically in orange sashes, dashing madly all over the place, mixing ourselves up with banner-bearers and bandsmen, and finally falling into the train as the whistle blew. There were always saucy girls on the train encouraging us to go with them to the carriages where the 'big kilties' from the pipe-bands sat, to find out how many of them were wearing trews under their kilts.

Over the years, the riotous outings merged into a general blur without detail except for a few occasions, such as when I could hardly walk in the procession. On the previous day I had been surprised taking flowers from a preparatory school garden, and a master had chased me for the best part of a mile. He never caught up, but the flowers cost me dear in the form of terrible blisters on my feet. For the outing I could not wear shoes, and set out in white plimsolls. In the train, someone took my overcoat by mistake and left me theirs which was too big for me. When we reached our destination I joined the march in a garment that came down to meet my plimsolls. The onlookers laughed as I trudged along in the pelting rain, holding on to a thick orange rope to steady our banner of King Billy on his white charger.

A sneaking feeling began inside, that perhaps the crowd's derision was well-deserved, for my odd appearance could hardly do credit to our cause. I tried to take my mind off it by concentrating on holding the banner steady, and listening to the band in front as it changed from *The Sash my Father wore* to *Dolly's Brae*, while the band behind bombarded us with:

> *On the green grassy slopes of the Boyne,*
> *Where King Billy and his men they did join,*
> *And they fought for our glorious deliverance*
> *On the green grassy slopes of the Boyne.*

The parade always included some Orange champion dressed in 17th-century clothes and riding on a white horse to conjure before our very eyes a vision of King Billy himself. But on the Easter Tuesday when I limped along in plimsolls the day's rewarding feature was to see the white horse rear up on his hind legs and throw the rider. He was a little, wide-moustached man, rather like the one in the famous 19th-century cartoon of Lord Randolph Churchill as 'King Randolph crossing the Boyne'. Off he went tumbling to the ground, his elaborate peruke flying. While two St. John's Ambulance nurses rushed to gather him up, we speculated on the certainty that the Mickeys had attempted an assassination.

Only one real assassination took place before my eyes on an Orange Easter outing. Some of my fellow Lodgemen from Sandy Row set fire to a hayrick and out of the holocaust dashed a rabbit. Better sport than hay-burning ensued, and in a few minutes the poor creature was dead, wounded from the things thrown at it and from the pursuers' boots. When the warm, furry football was left to go cold, and the louts went off in search of other fun, I gathered the rabbit up, happy to be alone so that I could bury it in a wood. I took the red-white-and-blue rosette from my lapel and gave the rabbit a good Protestant funeral. And in my heart I could not forgive the boys of Sandy Row for killing it.

Part of the day's thrill included leaning out of the train window to pick out which of the houses speeding by belonged to the Catholics. We could spot them easily enough for their gables, like ours, were painted. But the Mickeys' walls bore different signs—'Up the I.R.A.', 'Remember 1916', 'Silence is Golden'. The sign of the cross would appear on any blank space, and worse than any of them, 'God bless the Pope'.

The Pope! How we feared and hated him, we thought the Pope more terrible than Hitler when that German came to our notice, and certainly a greater evil than his disciple, Mr. de Valera. From the safety of the passing train we could boldly hurl abuse at the Mickeys' houses and their papish murals. Pushing to get a space at the compartment window we shouted 'To Hell with the Pope', a devout prayer on Ulster lips and a favourite one. As late as 1951 a member of parliament built a climax into an election speech with 'God save the King, and to Hell with the Pope'.

But God had not left us defenceless against the dreaded Roman Pontiff. He had sent us Lord Carson to secure our Ulster freedom. Lord Carson was dead, and when the C.L.B. parade brought me to St. Anne's Cathedral, I sat with great awe near the new tomb. He was another of the four-and-twenty elders mentioned in the *Book of Revelation*, and would be found sitting on God's right hand at the Judgement Day. The least religiously or politically minded knew about Lord Carson as did the fervent, and all knew the song,

> *Sir Edward Carson had a cat,*
> *He sat it by the fender,*
> *And every time it caught a mouse,*
> *It shouted, 'No Surrender'.*

Our rhymes were like calypsos, endless, ingenious if monotonous, and dealing with everyday events whether political or not. Whenever anything new happened, then we found doggerel for the occasion. Mr. Baldwin and an urging on to fight in Abyssinia appeared at one time. Mrs. Simpson became the theme of endless variations. How our mothers had idolized the Prince of Wales! And although pictures of the Princesses, Elizabeth and Margaret Rose, with their corgies in 'Y Bwthyn Bach', the Welsh cottage, now filled the photograph frames in the parlour, we could sense the survival of the liking for Prince Eddie. Often the only contact maintained with the exile was through the medium of the Sunday papers. We scanned the pages for scandal or pictures.

Reaction to any incident concerning Protestant or Roman Catholic was always violent, nothing escaped notice and comment. When the new king ascended the throne his was our forsworn loyalty. And yet, in spite of such entrenched opinion, our ignorance of the Catholic world was profound. I for instance, believed that Mickeys existed only in parts of Belfast and nowhere else except the Free State and Rome itself.

That many Catholics were living in London, or were allowed to live in London with our Protestant king, seemed impossible. The idea of a papist cathedral near the gates of Buckingham Palace would have been laughed at with scorn. So thought I, until Coronation year. The celebrations burst over the city like a great coloured rocket, exploding in the drabness of our lives with a million sparks, a spectrum of excitement. Belfast went mad with patriotism. Even the Plymouth Brethren so immured to anything but 'the word', published a coronation photograph on their Sunday tract.

Then we were presented with a magnificent coronation book, with close details of the ceremony, as well as pictures and diagrams of the important personages and Westminster Abbey, where it had all taken place. We prized the rare possession, and why not—for apart from religious story-books won as Sunday School prizes, hymn-books, and a vast collection of Bibles, New Testaments and Books of Common Prayer, it was the only real book in the house.

But through the coronation book I learned of what seemed a terrible betrayal. Included in the pictures of the royalty involved was one of the Duke of Norfolk greeting the two princesses. In a blood-curdling Orange sermon we heard about the subtleties of Catholic scheming, and the preacher had included Norfolk by implication. And there he was, a Mickey, shaking the hand of the heir to the Protestant throne, King Billy's successor!

But there were other, worse things of sinister import. Not only did he hold the office of Earl Marshal (we did not know what this was, but no matter) but he was head of the no-bility. If all the House of Windsor died, or were deliberately got out of the way, the Duke would be king, and the glorious freedom of Boyne Water would indeed be lost!

The Boys of Sandy Row

How I imagined Norfolk to be scheming and counter-scheming to win the crown, and send the country back to the days of Bloody Mary, whose history besides that of Protestant martyrs we had heard in school. Perhaps Norfolk would one day buy the confidence of a Buckingham Palace servant, who guarded the King night and day, and persuade him to steal the crown. I could see the vast, richly draped bedchamber, the Yeomen of the Guard, and tall plumed soldiers standing round the sleeping monarch, and his crown hanging on the end of his bed, next to his long underpants. The crown gone, life for us would be over. Was not that the reason why my mother, every year when the backyard was whitewashed, got a neighbour to freshen up the painted crown on the wall?

Such a pity for the lovely book to be spoilt like this. We would have liked to rip out Norfolk's picture and burn it, but this could not be done for the Princesses were on the same page and the King on the other side, and to remove them would be disrespectful. In fact, reflection showed it would have been disloyal, just as disloyal as the Mickeys putting their postage stamps on letters upside down as an insult to the Protestant throne. Instead, we gave the Duke a pair of horns and a nice tail with an arrow point sticking outside his rich coronation robes.

Unquiet Blood

Old Adam had tried hard enough. I suppose being a stern sea-dog on the high seas that was inevitable. His wife helped him as far as possible, and filled his quiver sixteen times. Presumably being worn out then, she gave up, but still had produced no son.

And what could Adam MacDonald do with sixteen daughters and no son? People who waited long enough saw him grow bitter, and add grumpiness to a reputation already including toughness and similar manly virtues. But roar as he might and terrify his sailors, and perhaps even the seas, into submission, the fact remained that he could produce no son. He knew, when thundering orders at the wheel on a howling night, or walking with his curious gait along the quay, that other men were thinking, 'For all his bluster, he can't get a lad'.

To cover the deficiency he took some of the daughters to sea and made them run up and down whistling riggings, pull on ropes and set sails, and swallow the destiny of a boy's life at sea. As a result the sixteen girls spoke in different accents, according to the place they frequented most, or rather the place from which their crew mates came. Some of the girls you would have sworn came from Lancashire, others from Wales, or even more outlandish parts. It must have galled the old man that his own rich Highland dialect was going to waste, and that never would he hear its inflexions first in the treble and then in the tenor of a son's voice. Perhaps some of this bitterness passed on to his daughters, for one of them was my maternal grandmother, and the rest my great-aunts.

By the time I appeared on the scene, it was much too late for old Adam to think of substituting me as a son. He was soon dead and quickly became a legendary figure in the dockland. But his daughters were still alive, though reduced for the greater part to being invalids and cripples. This, in itself, did not condemn them in my eyes, when I was old enough to distinguish one from another. Those I did hate were the righteous as distinct from the worldly great-aunts, for here, as in all else, the serpent of religion raised its ugly head.

Since the righteous ones had reluctantly looked after my mother when at the age of six she lost both her parents, the great-aunts deemed it their right to govern over family policy. They were puritanical fiends, ever ready to strangle the world, the flesh, and the devil with claws of hate, though it was proclaimed as a gospel of love. Sin was the green bottles under the kitchen sink, the billiard hall, or an innocent bit of dolling up the entry. God help the child who would stare at the kitchen pulley when the coms and bloomers were festooned, or worse, show a bit of bum. One sometimes wondered if God himself was not at fault in having given man a charley.

From the beginning they singled me out as a special object of their loathing, a feeling which I lost no time in returning. Not only were both my names those of my father, and my looks resembling his more closely every day, but they recalled how in his fatal illness, my father had clung to me. 'Leave him,' they had peremptorily advised Big 'Ina as my father's illness grew worse, 'Let the hospital have him.' And hearing of it, my father demanded that Big 'Ina was to go and take my two sisters with her, but not me. The idea possessed his wrecked mind and for weeks no one was allowed to take me out of his sight. This was stored up by the great-aunts, and long before I was capable of reasoning why, their hate focused its burning rays on me—all because I was like *him*, and was in fact, a second *him*.

Perhaps not all the sisters in the 'saved' branch would have been so vindictive, but at their head stood the dread figure of Great-Aunt Agatha. She leaned heavily on a stout stick, for a tram had tried to do justice and had knocked her down. My mother certainly never dared to carry face-paint or powder over that godly threshold. And the little plumber's mate never forgot the day, or the weight of the blackthorn stick, when he lit a cigarette while working on the lavatory after a freeze-up. No wonder, for the lavatory was a place of fear, and when I lived in the house, bouts of constipation lasting for days on end were quite usual. A row of religious books lined the wall, intended for lifting the mind to higher things while in occupation. On the opposite wall hung a calendar with a bulging stomach of a little text pad, each page with a date and Biblical quotation, one for every day of the year. And on the back of the door, lest the mind of the wicked should think unholy thoughts, was a fierce and lurid painting of an awful eye, with 'Behold the Lord thy God watcheth thee' written underneath.

The toll exacted from us by Agatha's interference and dictating of our affairs received only slender compensation. When my mother went into hospital I had to stay in Great-Aunt's house and suffer on earth the torments she wished on me in the hereafter. And that was the only help she ever gave, except to rip out the tops of her discarded grey stockings and re-knit the wool into hideous jerseys for me. During most of my childhood I wore these unspeakable garments, summer and winter alike. In my very first class at school a boy sitting near me, wore a blouse of claret silk. Its sheen looked so sumptuous when compared with my moleskin, that I had to slip behind him and touch it. Bobby Mathews, owner of the splendid blouse, became a sworn enemy of all my Belfast life, though whether because I fingered his blouse or not, was impossible to know.

Great-Aunt Agatha, like most of her kind, being more aware of sin in others than in herself, probably felt no twinges of guilt over her treatment of me, or over her diabolical behaviour to my mother as a child. Yet towards Cissy, almost as if in atonement, she displayed a partiality, that in anyone else would have been called affection. Only once did she ever reprimand Cissy. Sitting with her in front of the fire one day, Agatha asked my sister to sing 'Two little girls in blue'. But as she gazed into the flames, Cissy sang instead, 'Two little girls in blazes'.

'Enough' screeched Great-Aunt Agatha. The blackthorn swished menacingly through the air and out came the Bible story-books.

Great-Uncle Isaac, her husband, in contrast was beloved of all. And well the old witch knew it. She always contrived never to leave him alone when we were saying good-bye, and this was to prevent him from giving us more pocket-money than she allowed. Although in consequence Uncle Isaac was somewhat inaccessible, Big 'Ina always had the comforting thought that in a really tight spot she could waylay him, on his way home from work, for a quick quid.

It was Great-Uncle Isaac who brought the activities of the I.R.A. to my notice, for one day he was in the backyard when a parcel was thrown over the wall and hit him. He, of course, would not have associated with anything of that sort, and nearly all his time at home was spent in a corner chair by the glass-beaded curtains, flicking through the pages of an enormous Bible. He made copious notes for his sermons, for he was an Elder at one of the mission halls. While these profound studies were taking place we children were obliged to sit still, with suitable occupation, my sisters making dolls' clothes while I folded and rolled newspapers in a very complicated fashion to make firelighters. It was Uncle Isaac who made it possible for me to go to the orphanage holiday home in County Down every year. His blind sister, whose clever husband was also blind, belonged to yet another non-conformist sect that owned the home.

I hated staying at Great-Aunt Agatha's house more than anything else—even school. The gross Sabbatarianism that stalked its rooms was wedded to a stuffy respectability. Well furnished and carpeted, its inhuman perfection was maintained during non-praying hours by much polishing and cleaning. I disliked the spotless napkins and cork mats as much as the grace coldly said before and after every meal and snack.

Their pride in the house was impressed on me one day when I paid a surprise visit to the house. My sisters were staying there and I was boarded out with another great-aunt. Agatha was out and so I slipped into the glory-hole under the stairs, and on her return Cissy asked her to guess who had come to see her. She guessed immediately and also where I was hiding, for before I could come out she locked the door on me. When my crying and entreaties that I was dying in the small dark compartment were at last answered, I had to go into the yard and be inspected to see that I had no coal-dust or cat-dirt on me. Only then could I be allowed near the precious carpets.

The only pleasure in going to Great-Aunt Agatha's was the journey itself, for we had to pass the cattle-market and climb the long hill which led to the slaughter-house. Sheep-droppings covered the road and we walked in them to bring us good luck, and the smell brought the country into the town. On some days the sheep would be going up the hill like a cloud, their woolly bodies brushing heavily against me, and the trams islanded as the white mist filed by to its death. Our

Unquiet Blood

shoes alas had to be wiped clean of the good luck before we reached the house.

Agatha's hardened heart seemed stony indeed against Great-Aunt Emma's in whose house I also lived for short periods. Emma belonged to the 'saved' among the sisters, but was more kindly and understanding. She even allowed me a visit to the cinema once a week—the seat of the scornful!

But Emma, also, in her humanity was determined that I was not going to grow up like my father. To stop me from going about like a 'corner-boy' she had my trousers pockets sewn up. And because she knew that at home I liked to slip out of the house after being sent to bed, she made me share her bed over which Millet's 'Angelus' hung askew from a nail. Its calm impressed me deeply, but perhaps only because of the nervous tension in bed, which was its antithesis. I was confined to the side against the wall, to ensure that I could not climb out during the night. This was a certainty, for the poor old girl was paralysed down one entire side of her body. She could sit down on a chair, but had to be pulled up by somebody else. In bed, the night for me was a long-drawn-out agony, for if I fidgeted she screamed. The more I concentrated on not moving, the more I felt my limbs go stiff and wanted to shout myself.

The chief compensation at Great-Aunt Emma's, apart from the cinema indulgence, was the bread. Every day it was baked fresh (nothing so evil as Sunday baking took place), in stone jam-jars, and was made of a rough wheaten meal. The great-aunt earned a place in my stomach bigger than in my heart.

Like Agatha's, her husband was most agreeable, named Albert (no Bert-ing allowed) and generous like Isaac, slipping us many a wing when his spouse was not looking. Unfortunately, both for him and for us, he went to England for his sister's funeral, but fell down the stairs there, killing himself. He left Emma with an only daughter, who although crippled from birth was a genius at earning money from dressmaking.

In Great-Aunt Beatrice all breaches between the sisters were healed, for all were fond of her. She had been the old sea-captain's nestle-cock and darling, perhaps the only one he did not resent because she was not a boy. But poor Beatrice was slightly 'simple'. The sisters, the 'saved' ones, (Beatrice was an easy catch for the evangelical net) tried letting her live at their houses, but the experiment could hardly be called successful. Her condition deteriorated, her antics became more outrageous and so she had to be sent off to the workhouse.

She was a tall, eaten-away-looking woman in the grey workhouse uniform, with a disconnected imbecile emptiness about the face, framed by unloved brown hair. Once a month I went on an errand of mercy to see her, taking a quarter-pound of ginger snaps. She liked gingers, and received them with a puzzled, inquisitive, monkey expression. Conversation of any sort was almost impossible, especially for a child, for the points at which my chatter and her silence met were too few to allow of consecutive thoughts. The place itself made up in interest what Beatrice lacked, although even she took a more active part than most of her neighbours. She was not bedridden like them, and was employed on small jobs, including the disposal of bed-pans. Dozens of old crones crammed the wards, all in various stages of blindness, insanity and decay, and all had interesting histories behind them.

An ancient flower-seller who occupied the bed next to Great-Aunt Beatrice and who suffered from 'chill blood', always invited me to feel the unnatural coldness of her hands, which were like a marble statue's. I was present the day her son (a sergeant-major in the Irish Guards and whom I thought a demi-god) was clicking his booted heels in farewell, and the old girl climbed over the bars of her cot and wanted to go away with him in her big nightdress. It was a pathetic scene, to hear her crying and moaning, and see her being held down by the weighty wardens. Many of the women slept in these barred beds, to prevent their falling out, deliberately or otherwise.

During my ginger-snap visits I often met another of the Adam MacDonald progeny, and so far as looks went, the most remarkable—Great-Aunt Sarah. She was even taller, and more gaunt than Beatrice, and seen in the perspective of years, like a character out of an Irish comedy. Perhaps this effect came from the black peasant's shawl she wore, the only one of the sixteen sisters reduced to such conditions. Yet Sarah in her heyday had been the richest of them, through her first marriage. Now she wore the shawl and was doomed to live in a tiny house near the main gate leading into the docks. But at least she liked the sea atmosphere, for more than the other girls she had been the brightest deck-hand in her father's day, and her talk to me was of sailing ships. Old MacDonald's attempt at converting his girls into boys had met with some success in the mannish Sarah. She did not wear the shawl over her head in the usual custom, but round her shoulders like a cope. And on her crown of pure white curls she perched a man's cloth cap, that went with her everywhere. Hers was the Lancashire accent, broad and rich in humour, and of a humanity that altogether fascinated me.

Sarah and Agatha were opposite poles in the field of magnetism surrounding the great-aunts. Gossip said that Sarah was fond of the bottle and would suck whisky through a dishcloth. I could not blame her, not even if drink had been her family's downfall, though the details of an alcoholic history were never known. Sarah had more than her share of misfortune. After the loss of both her 'well-connected' husbands, Christy, her only son, went to work in a mill.

Christy's cleverness and handsome looks got him on the road to success and he was being trained to assume a respon-

sible position in the mill office. When he was fifteen, Christy
noticed a younger boy in the mill one day, pulling a great
load. He ran out to help the boy, and the sudden jerk from the
extra hand, made the stacked load come down on top of them
both. The younger boy escaped almost unhurt, but Christy
was terribly injured. His once-strong body was completely
deformed, his limbs made useless, his face disfigured, his
speech impaired so that he could utter nothing more than
gibberish. And the mill, so proud of him before, turned its
back on him and refused compensation on the grounds that
Christy had been injured doing something outside his duties.
The rest of his life he was to sit in a back room, an unwanted
monster.

Great-Aunt Sarah could perhaps bear this awful mutilation
of her son, because she still had Grace, her daughter. And
Grace's was the first wedding I ever went to as an invited
guest. I was five then. The whole clan submerged its differences
below an amicable surface and turned up in frightening numbers. Sarah took me into the room where the splendid wedding breakfast was spread out, and asked what I wanted to eat.
Dazzled by such munificence, my eye wandered up and down
the table, eventually lighting on a decoration set high on the
wedding-cake. Little imitation pearls of sugar surrounded it,
the whole thing looked delectable. But others present objected
and did not want the cake to be touched until the bride and
groom cut it with his military sword. They tried to entice me
away with éclairs and plates heaped with tempting diamonds.
But I insisted only the cake-top would do. Sarah, bursting to
spoil me, and no doubt thinking of her own son, lifted off the
decoration and gave it to me.

And this cake episode was pointed out as an evil omen,
and afterwards recalled as a pointer to the tragedy which befell Grace and her husband. They soon produced a son, who
by the time I had reached eleven was five years old, and him-

self already at school. He was called Capstack after his wealthy
English relations. He and I got on fine together. Then in the
playground one day, some bullies sat on him and gave him a
beating and little Capstack died. None of us was surprised to
hear the news that his grandmother, poor Great-Aunt Sarah,
steeped in sorrow and misery, was carried off to hospital,
gassed.

The great-aunts' fortunes dominated our horizon, perhaps
because there were so many, that wherever we turned within
the family circle, some were sure to be found. And the baleful
influence of the 'saved' ones could never be escaped. Yet they
were not our closest relations. My mother had a brother, Our
Danny, a romantic character who spent years of his life as a
soldier in the Inniskilling Fusiliers. A faded brown photograph of Our Danny and his pals in uniform was stuck in a
corner of the kitchen mirror. But his days of philandering
were over, and he got his discharge from the army, secured
himself a wife and a steady job as a road-mender. In spare
time he grew flowers—especially chrysanthemums—and if
the road-mending was near our house, he would come to see
us, bringing prize flowers with huge, exotic blossoms like
dyed poodles' heads. But his soldiering years caught up with
him, and while he was still young, delayed effects of being
gassed in the 1914 war killed him. He left one child, a daughter
blind from birth, who came to live in the institute beside us.

Calamity was the common lot of our kind. Hard and often
dangerous work, prolonged under-nourishment or over-
drinking, and the prevalence of bad health which bad living
conditions aggravated, made heavy inroads into all working-
class families. My mother's was no exception. Nor was my
father's. He too had a brother—Their Sammy. I never met
him until his daughter-in-law died, and I went to the wake.
The affair struck me as most impressive in a gloomy sort of
way, with candles burning near the coffin. Round the slender

wax reeds were paper collars printed with 'We mourn our loss'. And the girl in the open coffin looked like wax too, a wax doll with delicate features, perfect as if in life, except for the pallor. She died of IT (the gallopin' it must have been, for she passed away in her teens only a few months after marrying my cousin whom she most probably met in the sanatorium.)

The family did her proud with the wake; more ham sandwiches and meat pies than I had ever seen in a house before, crammed the tables. All the grown-ups were drunk, trotting back and forth between drinking at a makeshift bar, lined with ewers of porter, and peering into the coffin. Not the most sober among them was Their Sammy, who became involved in a bloody argument with one of his four fine sons. These boys early went to sea as merchant seamen or in the Royal Navy. They were heroes to me, and I would have longed to know them better, but was not allowed. My favourite went to jail shortly after the wake to serve a long sentence.

Their Sammy did not stay the course either, and long before old age, was taken from the bosom of his seafaring sons. Almost at once a caller came to our house—would my mother let them have the 'grave papers' so that Their Sammy could be fitted in? How ridiculous to ask, of course Big 'Ina could not. Surely they knew about there being room only for one adult or two of us children?

Because she lived in Canada and was also 'saved', a different attitude developed towards Aunt Flo, my father's sister. She was considered 'safe'—the distance could hardly have rendered her otherwise. But when the war came, one of her two sons turned up in Belfast, tricked out in naval uniform. I only met him once, and then his hands were in bandages. He had impatiently put them through a tram window, because the conductor took him past the stop.

Unquiet Blood

But his younger brother had forestalled him by many years, however, in attracting attention. Not long after my Aunt Flo and her husband arrived in Canada as poor immigrants, the Lindbergh kidnapping took place. As a newspaper story, it had a mixture of the best ingredients—drama and crime, human interest and sentimental appeal, and of course, it went on for months. The innocent Irish arrivals from Belfast were to be caught in the tentacles of publicity. While President Hoover and the Cabinet went into conclave, while the diplomats of Algiers searched for a baby dyed brown, while the police of Europe and Scotland Yard trailed after false clues, and while the world press was feeding its avid readers, all attention was suddenly laid at Aunt Flo's door. Her younger son was seen at the window of their poor home, and recognized as none other than Charles Augustus Lindbergh. Crowds became mobs, and collected angrily outside. Police flew in from New York. Meanwhile Mrs. Lindbergh had broadcast details of the child's diet, and the churches as well as the chaplain of Congress offered special Lindbergh prayers. Not until the real child's body was discovered face downwards in a ditch, could my cousin leave the house with safety. He fell ill with rickets a month after, but by then the tidal wave of sensational news had swept on to other topics. No one cared about the baby they had crowded to see at the window.

There is not a leaf of our family tree, either fallen or still green, but has been nourished by the rising sap of our unquiet blood. Every branch of the family yielded some fruit of passion or comedy, violence or tragedy. A curious gap in the tracery of family leaves occurs where Big 'Ina's and my father's parents should fit in. If ever they made a picture in my mind, it has since faded, and nothing remains but what photographs will recall. But *their* parents, my great-grandfathers and mothers, seem hardly to be dead at all.

Unquiet Blood

The Wee Lamplighter was already far advanced in his nineties when I first met him. Not even the great-aunts could keep him at bay, for our house had once been his, until he retired from lamplighting and went to live up the country. To work out exactly who he was, I had to count the generations backwards, starting with my father and then his father, until I arrived at the old man. Already his own son, my grandfather, also a lamplighter in his day, was dead, but the Wee Lamplighter had no intention of dying until he had seen out a full century.

And in this his wife, Great-Grandma, encouraged him. Removing a clay pipe from her mouth, the old woman would address him as 'Dick Man'. The decades had wiped away any trace of the wild beauty that may once have haunted her. All that they left was a wrinkled elfish face, which creased a thousand times when she chuckled, or gave a wicked kindly smile. She never emerged from a black shawl, which seemed large enough to envelop her frail body. It might be supposed that nearly a hundred years of life was enough to take away relish for it. But not Great-Grandma; the clay pipe she loved only came out of her mouth when she spoke or to allow black, stewed tea to go in. This was drunk from an enormous china mug with a portrait of Queen Victoria on one side and Balmoral Castle on the other. Like us, the old woman also had a great proclivity for pigs' trotters. Settled down by the hob, the trotters in her fingers, she was contentment itself, and made suitable noises as she sucked out the rich jelly—sucked rather than gnawed, for many years had gone since teeth stood in her gums. Whenever Great-Grandma came to our house she always brought us something to eat, and gave it to us with the recommendation that we 'Get it down yer wee craw'.

Her origins, being beyond living memory, were shrouded in mystery. Because she held anti-religious views and came from the country, and could swear in a strange language, people believed her to be a gypsy. The gilded glint in the hair that kept its oily overlay of colours until she turned the century, was taken as sufficient evidence of Romany blood. Others, less friendly, dismissed her as a mere 'tinker's cuss'. Nevertheless, whatever people thought of her, she was widely sought after, for she had the greatest charm in the whole of the six counties against the ringworm. Perversely, this was the only ailment common among us which I never caught, and so never had Great-Grandma to mutter her incantations over me.

As a pair, the Wee Lamplighter and his wife looked splendid, she with her shawl and pipe and he with a generous beard. How like General Booth's beard, people said, but the old man considered his flowing growth a far superior affair to the Salvationist's. This opinion may have been nothing more than prejudice, for neither he nor Great-Grandma became concerned with salvation until their lives' eleventh hour, and even then not until the midnight strokes were almost falling. After the Wee Lamplighter's ninety-eighth birthday, they went to stay with a grand-daughter, a 'saved' woman, who insisted on their going to hear a famous preacher.

This man was moving Belfast almost to the point of 're-vival', and thousands flocked to hear him every day. Old Dick and she set off and found seats. All went well until the Wee Lamplighter dropped a coin. His wife's ears, no doubt a little puzzled by what the man on the platform was shouting about, caught the coin's clink as it went down. She thought it was hers. The coin rolled with alarming loudness into the aisle, where it spiralled round and round, settling with a final clink. Great-Grandma and the old man dived after it at the same time, colliding on the way, and began to argue their respective claims to the coin. The evangelist could not stand such rival attractions, and the old couple had to leave the hall.

Unquiet Blood

Before they left the grand-daughter's for the country again, the Wee Lamplighter had a very nasty turn indeed. He went up to bed and undressed in the dark as usual, and climbed into bed. But something soft and warm had got into it before him. Reaching down between the sheets, he grabbed the thing, thinking it was some kind of animal, and flung it into a corner. The Wee Lamplighter had never known of a rubber hot-water bottle before, and did not appreciate his grand-daughter's thought for his comfort.

The old pair did not often stand inside our door, and I saw them more often at Aunt Becky's. Everyone in our neigh-bourhood resorted to Aunt Becky at one time or another, especially in sorrow, for greater than her reputation as a gossip, was that of making a first-class job of 'laying out'. She even did Mrs. Richie who was said to have had a steel coffin be-cause she was big and was expected to explode. Aunt Becky was not a real aunt, but only a cousin of my father's mother, who left Becky a copper kettle on a spirit stand and a thriving aspidistra, doubtless in the hopes that Becky would give her a good clean-up at her 'laying out'. The copper kettle shone like a setting sun in the middle of Aunt Becky's kitchen man-telpiece, and I was given a slip of the aspidistra to cultivate along with my ferns.

We thought Aunt Becky a very clever woman, for she could remember the number of wreaths at everyone's funeral for years back, and sometimes the names of particular flowers in the important ones. But being indispensable made her vain. Her hair was white, though profuse. It was also straight and this she could not abide. So one night, scorching hot curling-tongs were put into my hand with instructions to rectify nature's lack of imagination. I curled it all right—and roasted her neck into the bargain, dyeing her hair with burn marks of a particularly satisfying yellow.

She had a son, Ernie. Ernie did no work, and in consequence did not rise until late afternoon when he partook of a meal of stewed steak and onions that simmered perpetually on the hob. Ernie, however, could not be expected to correlate his actions with those of the more ordinary men I knew. He had been, once, a pianist of considerable talent and had given recitals over in England, a fitting achievement for the son of a well-known city organist. But something went wrong. He never could recapture his first fine raptures, they became more careless as time went on, and ended in his chief Belfast occupation of drinking. By thirty he had *delirium tremens*, by forty he was totally blind. I liked Ernie, chiefly because he had been my father's special drinking pal and provided me a link with him. When he was confined to bed I barbered him, fortunately more successfully than I had curled his mother's hair.

Because of Aunt Becky I became aware of the Jews. The small, hard core of hatred with which she regarded them, seemed incongruous in a breast usually so tolerant. Her niece had married a Jew, and this cast a shadow over the whole family, almost as bad as if she had turned to Rome. Anti-Semitism struck a strange note in the religious orchestration that clamoured for our attention. On the one hand, church and especially mission halls propagated the notion that Jews were 'God's chosen people', that Christ was a Jew, and had to enter the synagogue on the Sabbath. And at some services the collection went entirely to 'missions to the Jews'. But on the other hand, in everyday usage people referred to the chosen race as 'dirty yids', and in round terms deplored their custom of keeping Saturday holy instead of Sunday.

In imitation of my elders, and entirely without cause, I began to hate them too, particularly the man-with-the-three-brass-balls. Church, pub and pawnbrokers' hedged our lives about in an inescapable trinity, there were plenty of all three. The man in our neighbourhood who owned the biggest

Unquiet Blood

'Uncle's' was a Jew. His riches seemed to do him but little good for he was no more than skin and bone. We called him Inky Moses, inspired by the rhyme about 'The King of the Jews, who bought himself a pair of shoes.'

Inside the pawnshop, a stale stuffy dimness brooded. The long counter was divided into six or seven places by partitions, and so enclosed that it resembled a row of confessional boxes. The privacy of this arrangement encouraged even the most bashful to go in, for if a neighbour should happen to be present at the same time, the suit of clothes or the pocket-watch could be deposited in complete secrecy. Inky Moses himself always presided, dressed in a heavy flannel shirt, a waistcoat, and a once-white stiff collar, a bowler hat but no jacket. He made himself look hard-done-by and cultivated a pathetic expression to this end. But in fact, behind the bars of the confessionals, he was the hard one. The iron bars served to keep his merchandise out of arm's reach as though they were souls, and not brown-paper parcels, shoes, fountain pens and countless oddments, that were beyond redemption.

He seemed to traffic most in the ornate little medallions that men dangled from their watch-chains. He had thousands of them, as though he made it his business to snatch away the most precious and intimate articles. My mother disliked Inky Moses also, and would stretch things to breaking point, to avoid going. It was not always possible, the Sunday costume and even her wedding ring were sacrificed in the end for an occasional five shillings, which had to last until pay-day came round again. The wedding ring stayed so long once that it became unredeemable. I went often to the shop window to see if the ring was up for sale, determined to go in and ask its price, for Inky Moses did not sell cheaply. But the ring never appeared in the window—and then I was told why.

It was because of Inky Moses's wickedness, an evil of a particularly insidious kind. I learned that all Jews were saving up

every penny to go back and claim Palestine as their Promised
Land. And especially were they saving every ounce of gold.
The evidence could be seen in Inky's shop, where all sorts
of notices hung, requesting customers' gold objects, with the
emphasis on sovereigns. And when the Wee Lamplighter
died, had not his lovely gold watch, presented by fellow
lamplighters on his retirement, been sold to Inky Moses for a
song?

In the shop-cum-post-office almost opposite the pawn-
broker's I overheard a conversation between the postmistress
and a woman drawing her old-age pension. As she received a
crumpled ten-shilling note she remarked 'Och, t'would be
nice to see a bit o' gold agen, so it would, instead of all this
dirty paper.' The postmistress replied wistfully that there
was not much gold left in the country. And I could have told
them where it had all vanished to.

Once the Jews reinstated themselves in Jerusalem, they
would rebuild the temple. In the nearest Plymouth Brethren
hall to us, was a model of the temple building and I had studied
it. All the gold now being collected would be needed for the
new seraphim to guard the Ark. I even knew what the Ark
was like in detail—for on our gable murals, painted with
the other insignia, was the Ark and its winged, attendant
angels, exactly as it appeared in the masonic emblem of our
Orange Arch. Into these golden cherubim would be melted
my mother's wedding ring, the Wee Lamplighter's pocket-
watch, the sovereign Aunt Becky found between the floorboards, and the great hoard of gold medallions. How I hated
Inky Moses and (to my shame) chalked anti-Jewish slogans
on his wall.

Shadows

It was in the slit between the gas-oven and the wall, where the rats were supposed to get in, that I saw it first. The marks were blood, I knew for certain, and involved Big 'Ina in some way. The marks could only mean one thing—Big 'Ina was having terrible haemorrhages, but like all of us when we were ill, keeping it secret.

'She's bleeding to death, she's bleeding to death' a voice cried inside me, but I muttered aloud 'Oh God, I hate you . . . I hate you. . . .'

The more I thought about the awful facts, the more worried I became. I was going to lose Big 'Ina, but because of the secrecy I could not confide in anyone, or find comfort. I changed my praying tactics and confronted God with threats, 'If you let her bleed to death, I'll burn all your churches down. I will . . . I will . . . every Bible and hymn-book will go into the fire . . . I'll even join the Mickeys if she goes . . . wait till you see.'

Months later, I found new evidence of blood, and then again and unmistakably once again. Yes, Big 'Ina's got something, I thought in despair, and she's getting weaker and weaker. And this time I had not to wait long. We were sitting by the fire one night, Cissy was out pin-holing and Helen sat biting her homework pencil, and I was in a very bad temper because of having to eat porridge for my supper. Suddenly a slipping sound filled the room, followed by a thud. Big 'Ina had slumped to the floor, with her head in the fire. Quick as lightning, Helen pulled Big 'Ina's head from the grate, and I dashed next door for help, screaming at the top of my voice.

Always at their best in an emergency, the neighbours streamed into the house. I watched the smelling salts, the cold face flannel on her brow, and the brandy running down the lifeless lips. All failed to wake my mother. I started screaming again, big gasps and gulps of crying—all the fears of the last months were collapsing on top of me, drowning me, carrying me away. Several people tried to calm me, but I would listen to no one and had to be taken to the next house.

When the ambulance arrived, I had recovered control a little, but no one could prevent me from dashing out as they carried out the inert form on a stretcher. There she went, so ghastly; still unconscious—to me, dead. I would believe nobody who said otherwise, and I expected never to see her again.

Such a gulf of emptiness filled my heart when the doors of the great cream van were closed and the ambulance men dashed round to their seats, and drove off at top speed. The ambulance had come often enough to our house before, but always for one of us, never for my mother. Neighbours began to debate the immediate fate of the three stranded children, all under ten.

By next day we were distributed among the great-aunts. But I refused to believe what I was told about Big 'Ina. I had seen the blood, the terrible blood on the hidden vest, and knew she was dead. The news that Big 'Ina was all right, 'comfortable' as the hospitals say, could not possibly be true. If she was alive, why could I not go to see her in the hospital, in place of being told Bible stories and other distracting piffle? But all the same, just in case, I began to strike a bargain with God, 'If you bring her back I won't ever touch her purse again, I swear I won't ever say a bad word again, or chase the girls up the entry at night.' I got the Bible out, put my hand over it, and promised that if only Big 'Ina would come back, I would chop the sticks and light the fire every day. With a razor blade I cut my finger and signed a solemn agreement with God, concerning all the conditions under which I would live, if only Big 'Ina was returned to me.

And all this commotion over my mother was not filial devotion in the altruistic sense, but fear—fear that our home would be overthrown, and that I would be cast up on the shores of Great-Aunt Agatha's world for ever. Long periods had been spent there before, but this time the duration was unpredictable. I prayed to God most fervently, because I wanted to get away from the strangling atmosphere, and only prayed for Big 'Ina indirectly, as her health provided the key to freedom.

Previous stays with the great-aunt had all been after my bouts of 'trouble', and I was sent to be straightened out—a sort of brainwashing-concentration-camp treatment. And that is how I always regarded the place. Immediately I saw Big 'Ina in a heap on the floor, the realization flashed over me that it meant going off to Agatha's. I resented leaving my own home, where I had such freedom, as much as I was truly worried that Big 'Ina was dead.

Love of a less selfish kind must have been compounded in the strange mixture of feelings I held towards Big 'Ina. But it never appeared in isolation, and was never expressed in conventional sentiments. 'I'll do ya in', and 'I'll swing for ya yet', were ready words of annoyance in our home. No wonder my mother was frequently angry. Worn out with hard work, and harassed at home by a brood embodying all the worst characteristics of the family, she must have been exasperated beyond even normal patience at times. But her words of reproach meant nothing to us, so much water off the ducklings' backs;

we knew she loved us, slaved night and day for us, and that was enough. Only when the sleek, urgent ambulance clanged to the door, were we consciously aware that her presence in our lives was a necessity.

But we knew of her love by a kind of sixth sense for it entirely lacked overt, verbal expression. No terms of endearment like 'dear', and certainly not 'darling', were ever used. When I pleased my mother I was her 'own wee fella', and when in disgrace, which was more often than not, a 'flamin' sod'. Never would we do anything so soft as to kiss, for kissing was a mild form of 'dirty tricks' and belonged only to lovers up the entry. In all the years of my childhood I cannot remember my mother embracing me, even when I went away to the holiday home, or she to hospital. The only physical contact was in the very early years, before I was considered big enough to sleep in my father's old bed, on my own in the back room. Before this, in the cold nights of winter, my mother would wake up and ask me to snuggle close to keep her back warm.

God was interested in the terms I struck and sealed with my blood at Great-Aunt Agatha's, for Big 'Ina survived her collapse into the fire. And defying our fears she came back to pick up her life where it had been dropped. For a few days I kept my half of the bargain with the Almighty, and was very dutiful and obedient. But then Big 'Ina caught me putting my cod-liver oil and malt down the lavatory pan, and heard of my stealing apples from the barrow-boys. Out came the old razor strop and I was walloped, going for my mother in return, hammer and tongs with fists and boots, hating her and wishing she were dead.

But in the dead of the night, when I waited for the reassuring footfall in the empty street, contrition took the place of rage. Had it really been me wishing her gone? The pubs were shut, the neighbours locking up. Were they my boots that hurt her shins? The last tram rumbled by and as the sound receded the clip-clop of Big 'Ina's ill-fitting shoes knock-knocked on the pavements. I turned over and pretended to sleep. At least she would find me in bed as she peeped into the room.

Within a year the ambulance had called for Big 'Ina again, and even after this, and each time she stayed in hospital for longer periods. A suspicion, a mere pea on a drum, began to develop, that perhaps after all the connections between her physical condition and my moral one were not so intimately related, and that God, mercifully disinterested, did not in fact punish me by hurting her. And with partial release from this primitive fear came an acquaintance with hospital routine, and this familiarity bred a contempt for the ordinary person's awe of the building on the other side of the city. I was getting older and independent enough to find out from the porter's lodge how long Big 'Ina's name was on the danger-list.

And the terror of Big 'Ina's sojourns away from us was lessened, paradoxically, by the hospital itself. It gave us a reassurance of her love, from a source other than our sixth sense. Our knowledge about hospitals included many things to do with 'the knife' and the names of those who could best use it. We knew what anaesthetics were, and also that persons under the gas were apt to say things that in normal, waking life they would not dare to say. We had it that an evangelist from our district had sworn like a trooper in hospital, and several bad characters were reported as having called on the name of the Lord while unconscious. We noted all these sayings very carefully, for they were revelations of truth, not to be denied.

When my mother went to hospital, she always asked the theatre-sister, when she had recovered sufficiently from the operation, what she had called out under the anaesthetic. And the answer was stored jealously away. Eventually, when

we saw her again, she would shyly admit that while 'asleep'
she had mentioned my sisters and me by name. That was perfect proof and evidence of the way she really regarded us.
And it was sweeter than a thousand sloppy kisses.

Although rough usage hardened me and made me indifferent to a God who 'took it out of people', I retained the
instinct of fear. If life appeared to give you an advantage with
one hand, it took it away with the other. Whatever you
gained, had to be paid for. Getting older brought me priv-
ileges, freedom and a name for being 'bad'. So, obviously,
this had to be made up for, by suffering under Great-Aunt
Agatha. Being the strictest of the great-aunts, she was the
obvious one to deal with me. And living in her house was
made worse by the advent of my cousin Nathaniel.

He was Agatha's grandson, two years my junior, and had
just returned with his father to Belfast from Australia, complete with a flowery accent and a reputation for being good.
I hated him from the start. Big 'Ina was having another operation, and the worst two months of my whole life ensued
with this jinny. I would sit amid the highly polished museum
trying to keep my sanity by counting the strings of beads on
the half-curtains. I was once in such a nervous state, that when
folding up the newspapers for fire-lighters, I absent-mindedly
stuffed pellets of paper up my nostril. After a few days it began
to smell and hurt, no amount of poking on my part would
bring it down, and I, too, had to go in hospital.

But the tacky Nathaniel continued to shadow my life.
Agatha set us spelling-tests with catches like 'principle' and
'principal', and awkward ones like 'gnomon' and 'pneumonia'.
Then she totted up the marks, keeping me in suspense as
long as possible, while the horrible brat sat grinning smugly
at his *dear* grandma. Just fancy, Nathaniel has beaten you
again! And him *so* much younger than you! Aren't you
ashamed? Of course I was, but not over the spelling, but be-

cause of the ignominy Agatha deliberately put me to. I could
not even punch the silly Nathaniel's head as he was so much
smaller. With knitting it was the same, he could produce
yards of scarf while I still struggled painfully and unsuccess-
fully with a few inches of French-knitting through a cotton-
reel. I could see his genius, but was not jealous of it. I would
be disgusted to be like him, even if he might be able to make
his grandmother a pair of kneecaps by the time he reached
my age.

Before Big 'Ina went away and left me to be incarcerated
with Nathaniel, I made an important discovery. My friend
Tommy, from our street, had taken me into their house while
his parents were out. We had a good scout round the bedrooms, especially that of his maiden aunt, once my Sunday
School teacher. In her room I found another rag, blood-
marked like the one of Big 'Ina's I had seen behind the gas-
oven. But Tommy, in his worldly way, soon put me right.
All women had it, he said it was from the breasts and connected in some way (obscure at the time) with 'dirty tricks'.
What a relief to know that after all, Big 'Ina had not
been slowly bleeding to death, even before she fell in the
fire. And until the gang completed my theoretical instruc-
tion in sexual matters, I knew nothing further about men-
struation.

Nathaniel, wise child, had he my experiences would doubtless have profited by them. He would have learned that his
life revolved round his mother, and that deny the fact as he
might, it was nevertheless true. And if my cousin had possessed
an elder sister, he would have learnt that even she had a place
in his heart. Not being Nathaniel these truths eluded me most
of the time. Cissy and I fought every day. For her age she had
size and weight, and knew how to look after herself. She
used the weakness of her sex as the chief weapon, enlisting
Big 'Ina's and the neighbours' support, on the pretext that she

was only a girl while I was, metaphorically, a great hulking boy. Nothing roused me against Cissy more than her frequent use of taunts heard from Great-Aunt Agatha, scorning me and my father. Cissy always referred to him as 'yer ould da' as though he had not also been her own father. Arguments of this sort always ended in blows.

But fights with my sister were never conclusive, and she sought revenge. Her favourite method was to uproot my rose tree and ferns in the backyard, and hurl them over the palings guarding the railway. My retaliation would be to pull out as much of her hair as possible, or to ruin her homework after she had finished it and gone out. Or she would find my diary, where my most intimate thoughts were confided, and derisively declaim them aloud to the street from a bedroom window, while I was locked impotent with rage outside the house.

In spite of our spitfire relationship and the nuisance she could be, I harboured a fear for Cissy's life as I did for Big 'Ina's. In winter, when floods in the Bog Meadows froze, children flocked out to enjoy the new but all-too-temporary thrill of the ice. No one possessed skating boots, but this did not prevent sliding and all sorts of motions impossible on the narrow pavements and cobbled entries. Under our very feet, black, chill water waited to swallow the unwary, and this added to the thrill. My fears for Cissy lay here, for she ventured out alone to the thin ice, where it moved noticeably up and down under her weight. Hot spasms ran through my stomach as she ventured farther out, step by step, upholding her reputation as daredevil. We had been told in one of the mission halls about a man whose head was cut off by a jagged piece of ice as he fell through; it went spinning across the ice, calling out to be 'saved', while the unfortunate body drowned.

Came the spring, then Cissy and her friends found occupation elsewhere, this time up the grand Malone Road, on flower-picking expeditions. There, the gardens of the rich were ruthlessly plundered. Sometimes on these occasions she did not come home until midnight. Terribly worried, imagining she had been caught by the police, I would persuade my mother to let me get up, and go out to find her. This might be on the same day that we had quarrelled, when her school-books went out of the window in the rain, because she ate one of my pieces of toast, and when we had rolled on the floor lashing out and kicking, Cissy swearing 'by the bloody battle' to kill me.

Her failure to turn up after a flower raid made me more brotherly. In the darkness I would hear her clattering over the iron steps of the railway bridge laden with flowers. We were then the firmest of friends, hurrying home to arrange the booty in milk-bottles, as she confided the great dangers of the raid.

Big 'Ina strictly forbade us to steal, and well we knew the consequences of disobedience, but she did not mind flowers being brought into the house. Never for a moment did she think of them as being stolen. Apart from the one or two trips to Bangor, her world was the streets of Belfast. No wonder that for her the countryside was no more than a vague impression of open spaces belonging to anybody, and abounding with flowers and blossoms waiting to be picked. No desire to actually go into the country possessed her. Big 'Ina's peak of ambition was to spend a week in Blackpool, before, as she said, 'the Lord takes me'. She did not know much about flowers or their names, except sweet-peas, orange-lilies, roses and, of course, the fateful hawthorn, or any flowers connected with popular superstition. If I arrived home with an armful of the finest carnations, or bunches of lilac, and said I had picked them up in the woods, she never doubted it.

Shadows

One day, after a vicious quarrel with Cissy, she splashed the newly painted kitchen walls with ceiling-whitening. The blame, of course, would go to me. Weighed down with the injustice of life, I fled out of the house. When darkness came, and the gang dispersed, I climbed a factory roof and found a comfortable place between two of its sawtooth planes. Sheets of brown paper served as wrapping against the cold night and air chill but rich with the smell of new bread wafting from the nearby bakery. Light from the street lamp was hidden behind the roof. The stars seemed larger than usual, and frozen in their twinkling distance.

I believed the stars to be holes in the world's roof, where the glory of heaven could be glimpsed, and through which the rain fell. Years before, during a Sunday School prize-giving a rumble of thunder sounded menacingly overhead. But my teacher said that I should not be afraid, for a prize-giving was being held in heaven too. The lightning was only the flash of angels dashing up for their prizes, and the thunder-claps were applause from other angels, and I accepted this as a reasonable explanation.

And when I had grown older I knew the stars by name—local nicknames. The belt of Orion was the Three Struggies, and Sirius for us was the Fountain, for it spouted such fierce reds and icy blues. On clear nights I always looked to see 'My Bull'. But these nicknames were not invented in ignorance of the correct Latin ones, for those we learnt from the Sunday papers.

On Sunday mornings there could be no thought of church until Helen, Cissy and I had consulted the stars' forecast in the newspaper. After brooding over my own 'Taurus', I would follow Big 'Ina's 'Cancer', and then the stellar fortunes of the friends I expected to meet in church. An exchange system operated over these data. I collected their future from our paper and they studied mine in another taken at their homes. In this way I might have four or more forecasts for the week. Yet one more grudge against living with the great-aunts was the ban on Sunday papers, and the suspense of not knowing the stars' latest messages.

That night under my brown-paper coverlets, the smell of baking still crisp, I thought the firmament above looked blacker and fiercer than ever before. The crystal galaxies burned into my mind: were they really the worm-eaten floor-boards of heaven? I began to doubt the Sunday School teacher's astrology. The sky was spangled with star clusters so thick, that it looked like cow parsley in a celestial meadow; surely the angels must be mighty light ones to be treading on such thin boards!

Then from my eyrie in the roof, I heard a familiar voice reflecting from the buildings below—Cissy's. In our neighbourhood when anyone was wanted, people simply hollered at the top of their voice. Cissy bawled coaxingly, her tone tinged with anxiety, 'Robbie, come home, it's all right.' She had come to the waste site by the bakery, knowing it to be one of my haunts, though she would never have discovered me crouched on the roof like an earwig in an old brick wall. Reassured, I climbed down and as we went home, Cissy explained how she had cleaned the whitening off the paint before my mother arrived home from work; the damage had looked far worse in the moment of anger, than it really was. I could tell that my prolonged absence from home had worried Cissy, just as I worried about her late home-coming from flower-picking.

Cissy, firstborn, was Big 'Ina's favourite, as we were all aware. With Great-Aunt Agatha on her side as well, Cissy was infallible. People invariably took her word against Helen's or mine. Like us, she had also been 'delicate' in early years but was the first to be discharged, completely well, from the tuberculosis clinic. The beauty of Cissy's blue eyes was spoilt by a slight turn in one of them and this optic twist was the bane of my mother's life. To get the money required for a specialist, Big 'Ina spent extra hours on her knees, charring in the town. The battle of the turned-in eye went on for years but by the time she became a laundress at fourteen, Cissy could leave her specs off. Such a triumph went down as a red-letter day.

Very quickly, Cissy became a young woman, and already at twelve years she was big enough and sufficiently adult in behaviour, to share Big 'Ina's clothes. And they were always together. Helen and I were thrown on each other's company as a result, and never had the fearful fights that flared up with Cissy.

For Helen's first year at school, she had me as protector to and from the infants' gate, as I held her hand and took her safely across the roads. At night, since we slept in the same bed and went up before the others, we shared our secrets, and disclosed things kept hidden from Cissy and Big 'Ina. By putting the pink flannelette sheet over the knobs and twiddly bits of the brass bedstead, we made a cosy tinker's tent and curled together underneath for the whispers in confidence.

But it was the same pink sheet that caused a prolonged dread in me, years before I found the blood marks behind the gas-oven or in terror watched Cissy venturing over the dangerous ice. Helen slept with the bedclothes round her head like a shawl, and often made a complete mole of herself. Calling out 'good-night' to us Big 'Ina always told Helen not to bury herself under the coverings. She warned her in a serious voice she used when worried, 'Ya'll suffocate.'

Suffocate—a frightening word, a weird disturbing disease to catch, not a straightforward one like the falling sickness, or scabies, or even IT. Helen suffocate, that was an awful fate I had to guard her from, waking in the night to see that she still breathed. And even when I left the big brass bed and went into my own in the back room, I sometimes crept into the other room to save her from the strangest of all the diseases that could kill us.

Helen's best friend was Florrie Johnston whose brother Willie had sponsored my name with the Loyal Sons of William Lodge. Johnston seemed the most common name in the neighbourhood. Teachers and clergy had the name Johnston. There was Johnston the paper-hanger and Johnston the piano tuner, Sam Johnston the grave-digger and Joe Johnston the racing fancier. Another was a banner artist who painted his Johnston father as Moses whom we recognized when the banner was carried in the Twelfth procession. Then we had a churchwarden Johnston whose weekday calling was that of coal merchant, though superior to those who peddled compressed coal-dust bricks by ass and cart.

Churchwarden Johnston boasted a brass plate on his three-storey house, a large dray-horse and a wife who sang in the cathedral choir. But even such possessions and grandeur as those could not compare with the Johnston brothers who kept the riding stables at the end of the Lisburn Road, for their mother had been none other than *the* Mrs. Johnston, the dam of twenty-one sons. Nobody could deny that this prolific mother was the most notable of all the Johnstons, a recipient of divine favour. Such plenitude must have made poor Great-Grandpa MacDonald smart with jealousy. Even the quality remembered her. But I could not recall seeing her though her memory remained untarnished. And Mrs. Henry herself, the doctor's wife, declared that the proud mother of twenty-one sons had walked up the Magdalene Church aisle on a Sunday like a duchess, as, indeed, she had every right.

Lough Neagh Summer

Mill chimneys, caked under their black lichen of smoke, phallic obelisks pointing in mockery up at heaven; the streets where lived thousands of sweated labourers, ranged in fearful geometry, row upon wretched stillborn row, and an outcrop of crude civic buildings, bloated into ugliness by the so-called city fathers of the last century; these were the core of Belfast. To decaying Protestantism, Belfast was a place of pilgrimage, a Mecca of Orangemen. Misery and darkness for the many; quick money for the few. Unloved children, old women rotting in dirt under their shawls, I knew as Keats and Hippolyte Taine knew. Since they wrote of the city's horrors times had changed little. Festering scab are words which described it well enough.

Mercifully, this was only a sore in our otherwise green land. Where its walls stopped, the fields began, running almost as if bricks and mortar chased them, to the mountains, and there reared up defeating even the omnipotent mill chimneys. The majestic, purple presence of the hills could be felt, and every dismal chasm of a street gave glimpses of a rounded hump or a blue, distant shoulder. Sometimes smoke or rain blotted the mountains out, drawing a drab pall over the city. And then, when the clouds cleared, they would reappear, comfortingly near, suggestive of wild cotton moors that stretched on the uplands behind them. There lay a world of

the dog-fox yelp and the crying of God's goat. The folds of
those hills echoed with Neeshy Haughan's laughter as he
mocked the dank, sparse notes of Friday's pay-packet with
the jingle of his gold.

But it was neither gold, nor the doctors' repeated warnings
that without plenty of fresh air I would surely die, and my
mother's consequent insistence that I must always be out,
that drove me into the countryside. Rather, I was drawn.
Strong, invisible cords pulled me from the city and bound
me to the hills and streams and woods. A clarion rang out,
and I answered it.

Inarticulate at the time, these feelings expressed themselves
in an irresistible urge to get out and away from the streets.
Any means that came to hand were good enough. The slow
cattle-wagons rumbling and clinking along the railway lines,
now became a necessity; the element of thrill in stealing a
forbidden joy-ride dwindled away. Until then, my boon
companion had been the broken stump of a briar pipe; but
now I neglected it, the haze of forbidden tobacco smoke, once
so luring, began to thin as the drumlins of Down loomed up;
the mountains of Antrim and the sacred hump of Slemish
where St. Patrick herded the swine; the magical mirrors of
Lough Neagh and the pink-coiffed orchards of Armagh; and
the great oozy sloblands of the winter coast speckled with
redshanks and mudlarks. My poor whooper-swan returned in
spirit, white, more beautiful than before, his brave wings no
longer fowlers' prey, but powerful and free to bear me away.
My Bog Meadows, once so vast and full of wonder, gave
place to a wider world of pastures and bursting mountain
streams.

The thrill became more intense than before in travelling
out to those remote moors. I took to riding on lorries' tailboards, or if lucky, a cattle-driver down at the slaughter-
house might be persuaded to carry me out into the country.

Lough Neagh Summer

At each journey, inwardly I trembled, almost unable to keep my quivering excitement secret.

I always went alone; this was essential. The gang had no objections to orchards for they could be stripped of their fruit, nor to birds for they could be pelted by catapult. And in summer the sally-bushes as a jungle to hunt and fight in could be improved upon by going out to camp in the country, not because the gang thought nature as beautiful, but because there they could be absolute masters of time and of the pleasures to fill it.

But the gang had certainly no patience for jinny-slop like flowers or merely watching birds. And my precious binoculars must needs be protected from Gandhi, he would only see in them the shilling or two they would fetch at Inky Moses's. To focus my glasses on grey phalarope or mackerel cock along the Lough, I had to be alone. And how, in a crowd, could I have tried to read the wordless meanings of spoors, printed with such delicate hieroglyphics in the ermine of raw winter snow?

I drowned in the rapture of summer, and even in my innocence understood that it was sensuous, voluptuous. But I did not love its Pan-magic more than autumn or winter, perhaps even less. The foot-writing of weasels and badgers on the damp earth hypnotized me; even January, bleary of sky, seemed blithe when song-thrushes and the wilder music of the snaw cock chimed among the bare branches. Before a cold sun rolled down behind the hills on afternoons that died at four o'clock the dipper would sing, and blue and great tits. Delightful linnets would break forth in the French-fuzz, so nutty and warm to shelter in against the fierce storms. The French-fuzz's yellow fire defied even the coldest days, and dog-roses glowed like live coals with their vermilion buckieberries.

I collected buckie-berries for an aged woman who had once

lived in Devon, and whom fate had brought to our mean streets. Mrs. McClellan, as she was called, always encouraged me to bring her a few cuttings and roots of herbs and flowers. We imagined she put the buckie-berries down her fat husband's back as an irritant. He loved sleep, but unfortunately was obliged to earn a living by being a watchman at the match factory. He could often be discovered at the local bonder's, snoring loudly over his empty glass. We guessed she wanted to keep him awake, otherwise he would have to join the swelling concourse of the unemployed.

Mrs. McClellan asked me, also, to collect herb Robert, which she called Dolly's apron. Afterwards, as an evacuee in Fermanagh, when I saw herb Robert collected to cure cows suffering from the red water, I concluded the old Devonian had used it for similar purposes.

In return for the herbal presents she allowed me top priority in claiming her 'ould skins'. Our entries resounded with their own street-cries as inimitable as the cherries and lavender of London. And ours would have been incomplete without the cry of 'ould skins', just as fill-dike February would have been incomplete without the yellow yorlings' and corn buntings' songs. 'Ould rags, jimpots an' bottles' intoned the rag-man. A rap on our back door might mean that somebody wanted to collect our potato peelings, 'ould skins'.

Kitchen refuse was sold to a neighbour who kept, miraculously, thirty pigs in a backyard. The pathetic squealing of the pigs as he got them ready for the slaughter house, and the cries of the entries formed harmonies embedded in the music of my earliest years. Pig swill providing a potential source of income, I often took a bucket myself and trudged from door to door, 'Any ould skins, missus?' to earn an odd penny or so from our neighbour. What a memorable day it was, when two of the pigs escaped and raced blind with fear and panic down the street.

Lough Neagh Summer

No shadow of doubt obscured the fact that Mrs. McClellan was *grande dame* of the neighbourhood. What with her swanky Devon accent, the chiffon neck trimmings, and pendulous amber jewellery, she commanded awe. Her glory, however, suffered one defect—her poor feet, which bunions and corns knotted and contorted to a cruel degree. Mrs. McClellan was not above asking a neighbour in, to play about with a razor blade down below, while she affected nonchalance and read tea-leaves. She was great at the cups.

Such qualities alone would not have rendered Mrs. McClellan so queenly in our eyes. The car was responsible for that, and not a go-car, either, of the sort that usually fetched home a miserable half sack of coke. No, hers was a real car, though only a Baby Austin. To us, it seemed the epitome of riotous living. And the old woman was not insensible to its social value, and though they rarely used it, made sure that the car received a regular twice-weekly cleaning and polishing.

Sometimes I helped with the cleaning of the Baby Austin, and got myself taken on outings. The excited state that their first invitation brought me into, seems scarcely credible now; rocketing to the moon is not to be compared. Lough Neagh was fixed as destination, and I nearly swooned at such fulfilment of dreams. In the back of the car I sat with a broomhandle sawn into four, pieces destined to be thrown into the waters of the Lough.

Lough Neagh hones! Lough Neagh hones!
You put 'em in sticks and you take 'em out stones.

The lake's petrifying properties were like an article of faith to us, and even the science teacher at school believed that pieces of wood thrown into the waters and left for seven years would turn into stone. The seven years, I suppose, derive from our general superstitions that the numbers three and seven governed life.

Lough Neagh Summer

How I contained myself in the car until we arrived at the great lake, remains a mystery. Perhaps I was afraid that without utmost haste the fishermen would go, and I would not see their legs. From standing in the water with nets, their legs were supposed to be so hardened that they could hone razors on their shins.

Mrs. McClellan added to the suspense I suffered by prolonging our journeys with frequent stops. Did I want to 'make my water?' she would enquire in her luscious Devon accent. I fancy this concern was not for my comfort but for their precious car. Curled up and shaken about in the tiny back seat as I was, she probably feared for the effects on the upholstery if I should wet my pants.

Even on the shortest trips several stops had to be made; the subject so possessed Mrs. McClellan that it was no wonder I had to bring her herb Robert from my own wanderings. Her fears may have been a presentiment, for one day the dread thing happened. By a queer twist of fate, I was not the culprit. Mr. McClellan left us in the car while he called at a shop. Hardly had he slammed the door and mingled with people on the pavement, when the car began to run slowly forward, for we were on a slight rise. All that nerves and a weak bladder could do, they did at that moment to Mrs. McClellan. Heroically I flung myself into the front and heaved on the brake. I thought the old girl would die, and when our panic subsided she was in such a state, insisting, between gasps, that she must change there and then!

Lough Neagh disappointed me on the first visit. In vain I looked for hills and mountains to cloak it in the grandeur seen by my mind's eye. When we emerged from the tiny car, in which the sun had fairly cooked us, swarms of flies circled in buzzing haloes round our heads. Mrs. McClellan fanned herself with a lace hanky and declared she could not stand it, and all I could think of were the Biblical plagues about which, for no obvious reason, we had been taught in school.

But I refused to be put off, suspecting that the unromantic Mrs. McClellan had something to do with the disappointment. Afterwards, I went on my own, and quickly made friends with the fishermen. Their business in the great waters, the lake and its ten rivers, concerned eels and pollen, which were sent to London. The idea that Londoners ate eels filled me with disgust, for it seemed no better than the French swallowing frogs and snails.

Mrs. McClellan ate them too, though we excused her this particular oddity on the grounds that she was English and therefore liable to do peculiar things. The consuming of the slimy things however did not seem to us so strange as the way in which she hung up their skins by the kitchen hob, where they dripped oil into a saucer. For what black-magic or perversion she used this we could only guess.

We all loved Mrs. McClellan's extravagant character. To her, everyone was 'dearie'; milk-boy and long, thin curate, who thundered the streets on a motor-bike, were not distinguished by rank. Whether we approved or not, and we usually did, 'dearie' it was.

I liked her not least because she taught me many things from her considerable knowledge as naturalist. She gave quaint Devon names to everything. Although this did not lessen my avaricious grasp for information, what she taught was difficult to change afterwards. So for me, fool's watercress was always pie-cress, foxgloves always flop-a-docks, sundew always fly-catchers, besides a host of others.

Mrs. McClellan had a soft spot, as she said, for flop-a-docks, and whenever the Baby Austin rattled us home from an expedition, we would keep a look-out for some to pick and take back to the city. A man of the sea, Mr. McClellan preferred the coast country when he could draw his wife from the moors and mountains. We did not need to drive far from Belfast before finding romantic shores, where we took picnics amid a peppered carpet of sea-pinks, bird's foot trefoil and lady's fingers.

Of all the Baby Austin's outings, those to the sun-blazing or mist-shielded moors were the best. Unfathomable mysteries to me were the soft dove-tinted cloud-shadows mirrored in the bog pools, the light dance of tiger moths over the cotton grass, the secret life of the moss-cheepers amongst the heather and ling and the heavenly bog-myrtle. But most profound of the mysteries were the mountains, remote and softly coloured with ever-changing charcoal blues and purple greys. Their outlines were never harsh even when threatening rain cleared and sharpened the air, bringing every fold into detail. But nearly always, silvery clouds shot with light hung about them or swept veils of rain over them, obscuring the kind hills and their green, pleasant pastures.

Mrs. McClellan went in search of her fly-catchers and steep-wort to replenish her quaint pharmaceutical stores. Big fat Joe trailed behind, unable to relax amid the splendours for the fear haunted him that his beloved's good Devon hams would sink and be lost for ever in the bogs or hidden springs. And up on the moors when we went blaeberrying, during the autumn that shed gold over the vast landscape, I saw my first crane. Out of a small stream it mounted the air in slow motion on great wings, leaving me quite bewildered.

Loneliness was essential for wanderings in the country. But when in the mood for company, I really preferred the gang to Mrs. McClellan. In spite of the glory associated with the Austin, a glory which grown-ups besides children coveted, I preferred the long trek on foot, especially when the novelty of jaunting in the car had worn off.

From somewhere, the gang's younger boys procured a tent. With a ragged assortment of equipment we set out, undaunted by a trudge of miles that lay ahead. The tent's capacity bore no relation to the actual number that crowded into it at night-fall. We swanked about how many occupants there were on the previous trip. This boasting compensated for the discomfort. However brave and daring we thought the whole thing, the tent's fetid atmosphere would hardly be called attractive. First we choked the air with smoke from cigarette stubs harvested out of the gutters, and after an hour or so, the combined heat of our bodies and feet dusty from the trek added to the effect.

In the summer and early autumn, when my mother judged the weather to be good and allowed me to go, the nights were short-lived. None of us thought of sleep; that was a silly thing invented by parents to get you out of the way. We went camping for the fun, especially the making of a fire and gathering round it while night cunningly took possession of the forest. The scarlet glow and the saffron tongues of flame lit up our faces. In the vast silence that reigned among the trees, the sizzling and crackling of the damp wood seemed enormous. And we might hear the distant babbling of a stream gushing endlessly through the stones of a dam we had made earlier in the day. And in that hour, out of the velvet stillness, fell the nightjar's mellow churring. But the reeler, as we called it, penetrating the aisled woods from the meadows beyond with a throbbing music, was not so prevalent as the corncrake. His harsh cry, grating inharmoniously, comforted me strangely. In some way it was more homely than the weird reeler.

We told and listened to ghost stories, interminable and quite untrue, our sole aim being to pile horror upon horror. And then, half-believing what we had heard, gave the fire a last stir so that a fountain of golden sparks shot up, and scrambled into the tent. Not however to sleep. Around the fire we had been paragons of decorum, but now we began tumbling and tussling, wrestling and writhing, entwined in a heap of panting young bodies. This might go on for hours with a pause each time the tent collapsed on top of us, the crowning delight. Eventually sleep would overtake us. First one would be discovered, sprawled in a corner deep in oblivion, then another, until even the staunchest opponent succumbed to the stealthy stealer of time. Then the heat of our exertions would dissipate and the night cold enter our bones, and half-waking we would huddle together for warmth under the scanty bedding.

The woodlands were astir with half-moons, willow-warblers and siskins. The cooing of pigeons filled the groves with arcadian music, a pedal note which held together the whistlings and pipings of countless other singers. Being in the gang's company, my passion for bird watching could not be indulged. Instead, we occupied the days by racing through the forest or across green fields, free as the sky above was wide.

We cloaked our freedom under such guises as playing savages or Indians, and flinging off our clothes we tracked and pursued each other through the undergrowth. We dashed yelling down a grassy slope, feeling the sun's embrace on skins whitened by the city's darkness. Then plunging into the wood again, we sank like fish in the green submarine shallows of bracken.

To Shaw's Bridge spanning the placid Lagan, we most often bent our steps. Not much more than a mile lay between its graceful 17th-century stones and the last clutches of Belfast, yet enough to keep the milling throng away. On Sunday night it was, however, a paradise walk for lovers and a hunting ground for peeping-toms. Our curiously assorted camping equipment could be taken there without too much trouble. Besides, woods rolled over the gentle slopes, enticing the young savages by their cool beauty.

Usually we kept to one particular wood where limes and beeches, tall and nobly limbed, let freckled sunlight filter to the ground. I reverenced these trees, though with a feeling I could neither recognize nor express. Birds could be watched and flowers picked, but what could be done with trees? Because there was nobody to explain their loveliness, I joined the gang in one of the few devilments I got up to while in the country. Many of the trees were burnt out at the heart from campers' fires and we also thought it great sport to burn out a trunk and use the blackened hollow as a cave. In spite of our vandalism the trees survived; as we returned each year I was surprised to find myself changing more than the beeches we tried to destroy.

The murmuring Lagan dashed itself over weirs below the bridge, and here the boys of Belfast came to swim. The thought of plunging in the cold water did not appeal to others in the gang, for they could not swim, and we supposed that treacherous whirlpools and currents lurked under the smiling surface.

I, at least, felt envious of those youths who flung themselves into the deep river, and held races up and down. I would stand in awe on the bank, and watch as they moved powerfully in the water, or as their muscles tensed like taut springs before they dived. It seemed impossible that I would ever grow as strong and handsome as they looked when they clutched at the banks and heaved themselves on to the side again.

Slightly comforting was the thought that although I could not swim, yet unlike the rest of the gang I had been in the sea. At the orphanage in County Down I bathed happily inshore, careful always never to let my head go under. Fear of drowning derived from a bad moment in a swimming bath, when boys of a rival gang threw me in at the deep end, an episode concluded with artifical respiration.

The waters of Lough Neagh were destined to see my baptism as a swimmer. Big 'Ina's baby had grown by then to a long boy of twelve. He did not know at the time, but that summer by the Lough was to be the last before he left Belfast altogether. As I lay near the lake edge scanning the reeds and sky with my binoculars, no intimation of great changes dimmed that perfect world. Life contained no surprises. None except Eoin.

The oyster-catchers dabbled about, all unconscious of being watched. And then some inexplicable sense warned me that I too was being watched. I sat up, binoculars hanging from the strap round my neck. He stood there, just looking with dark eyes. About the husky figure a rough animal quality clung, a kind of glow that I knew our men of the city never possessed. I could tell he belonged to the fishermen for over a rugged, powerful figure a blue jersey was stretched. Big biceps threatened to burst the rolled-up sleeves when he folded his arms, and scrutinized me.

At first he said nothing, but when he eventually brought himself to speak, I immediately felt superior. In spite of the handsome face and raw health, he was a mere bumpkin without an ounce of gumption. He imagined I was a spy. A nod in the direction of the binoculars, explained everything. At that time the thought of spies possessed everyone. War-clouds rumbled on the horizon and any unusual activity roused suspicion like Lough Neagh's flies round the person concerned. And my lack of a Belfast accent convinced him.

To be taken as a spy pleased me immensely. That I, a mere cub of twelve, could hoodwink a fully grown man increased the vanity I already felt at looking much older than my age. Certainly better than the girl on the Sunday cruise. Coldly, I informed him that I came from Belfast, the right quarter of Belfast. This satisfied him and he flung himself on the grass, telling me his name—Eoin.

Haughty and superior I decided to be to this fisherman, who for all his twenty-five years or more had never travelled on a train and worse, had never been to Belfast. But my attempt to confound and embarrass rolled off him, my big talk about the city and the Baby Austins that we all owned left him unmoved.

Instead he began slowly to pull off the coarse jersey. 'Are ya goin' ta swim?' he asked in a friendly way. I suddenly felt that he regarded me now as nothing more than an unusual fish brought up in his net. The spy glamour dropped away and left me feeling awkward. I tried to gather shreds of dignity together. 'No' I replied to his question. I would have died rather than let him know I could not swim. 'Besides' I added, on the defensive again, 'I've got no costume.'

He laughed, and unbuckling his belt, let his thick trousers fall to the ground and stood in his bare buff. I had never seen a naked man before. In the gang we had no false modesty and were quite accustomed to seeing each other's thin undeveloped bodies. But a fully grown man seemed different. Eoin's magnificence; the roundnesses and hollows that his jersey had concealed; the muscles running across his back and shoulders like spring lambs in a field, when he swung windmill arms round, filled me with wonder and astonishment. With an inner ear I heard the great-aunts scolding me for daring to look at the young Adam's back, all the horror of nudity grating in their sharp voices.

Eoin, knowing nothing of the confusion he had put me to, ran with great strides down the slope and flung himself into the water. Birds flew up and ring upon ring of ripples spread across the lake. He called, but I could not distinguish the words.

Out of the corner of my eye I saw him approach the shore again and climb on to the grass. His footfalls made no sound as he came dripping towards me. I pretended to take no notice as he stood in the sun to dry himself. As I looked at a part of the sky where no birds flew, I heard his hard breathing, and deep gasps of satisfaction.

Lough Neagh Summer

Then he started to talk about the oyster-catchers, or fish rooks as he called them. The white cross on their plumage, he said, served as a memento of the night when these birds found the Lord Jesus Christ on the seashore. The high priest's soldiers were on their way to arrest Him, and so the fish rooks concealed His sleeping figure under a covering of seaweed. And the sacred token was given to the birds as a reward.

I regarded him in amazement. First at the story, and then that he should tell it while standing stark naked, all without the slightest feeling of shame. Then as he turned towards me I gave up the pretence of searching the sky for birds and looked at him. Immediately I noticed the terrible sign—a tattooed Sacred Heart garlanded with shamrocks. A Mickey—he was a Mickey!

I could hardly believe I had been cornered, helpless with a dreaded Mickey. But on and on he talked about birds, and the first impulse to get up and run left me. But I could not take my gaze from that tattoo; it hypnotized me as though to cast an evil spell over my stout Orange soul.

As Eoin went on telling me things I had never imagined about the birds teeming by the lake, my glance wandered in curiosity over the mass of that muscular mountain. Exertion had made him hot and the ruddiness of his skin showed up the black glossy waves of his hair. Altogether Eoin was a hairy creature, from the thick raven locks and unshaved chin to the profuse crop that raced in unbroken contours down his solid-looking thighs and legs. Only the red tips of his nipples and the Sacred Heart, pierced through the thicket on his chest. The rugged grandeur of his physique filled me with a strange feeling I had never experienced before. Awe and fear were compounded in it, for I realized he could overpower my feeble body by a single blow.

Eoin suddenly became conscious of my gaze. He abruptly left the subject of birds and asked, casually, if I was going in the water with him. This invitation, I concluded, was meant to decoy me, and that behind those haunting dark eyes, and those lips parted in a generous smile, lurked a cunning Fenian waiting to drown a Billy Boy.

When he had gone away, dry and glowing, a heavy sadness descended on the afternoon. I was even disappointed that he had not tried to frighten me with his knife because I had told him the number of my Orange Lodge before I had seen the tattoo. Countryside that had carried the burden of early summer so well while he was there, took on a drab appearance. In spite of the fear involved I wanted to see Eoin again. He had told me he went every day to bathe there, and during the weeks following this first encounter I schemed nefarious ways of mitching school, and of getting lifts out to the Lough side.

The mist of my fear dispersed in the sun of his friendliness and a bond sprang up between us. Glorious hours flowed by more sweetly than the Lagan as we lay silent in the grass listening to the lake birds' cries. I knew the father I had lost was found, and that the brother for whom I had longed so many times, the friend I dreamed about, the teacher I could respect, were all summed up in the good Eoin.

Ravenously I devoured everything Eoin could teach me. The slow, almost half-wit delivery of his speech belied a vast knowledge of the country, and the quickness of an eye that constantly searched the open sky, the tall reeds, and the lake depths, where his fine body dived and darted as though changed to a fish.

Swimming and playing about in the water become associated with him in my mind, as much as bird-lore, but a long time passed before I divulged the terrible secret that I could not swim. The day I told Eoin he did not scorn or laugh at me as I feared but gently said he would teach me. Even so I postponed the moment when my jersey would have to come off

179

and his eyes in turn look at the undeveloped scantiness of my
body.

Nevertheless the evil day came, and I undressed, trembling
inwardly. It had not occurred to me that unlike myself, he
thought nothing of these things. In infinite patience Eoin
showed me how to control my breathing, and one morning,
when this had been achieved, he took his arm away. I was
alone, treading the water, unable to touch bottom. The calm
look in his eyes, floating only a few feet from me, stilled the
rush of panic.

Eoin instructed me to imitate a dog paddling in the water.
In amazement I felt buoyancy keeping me up like one of the
swan-winged angels. Slowly the paw-paddling edged me
forward, until I closed the dread gap between myself and
Eoin. I rested my hands on his shoulders, and then set off
again, returning for another rest to the rock-like island of his
body. Soon I was as happy and free in the water as he; and
though now I am a strong swimmer and can go long distances, the dog-paddle survives.

Halcyon days like those could only be snatched once in a
while; school and its sterile nonsense required propitiating,
and sometimes my system of pick-up transport out to Lough
Neagh failed completely. That was bitter irony. Consolation
came from the fact that Eoin too needed to work to justify
his existence in a demanding world.

More often than not, choice lay between the gang's company or none. But now my solitary roaming took on a deeper
significance; the observing of birds and the collecting and
pressing of wild flowers assumed urgency, for they provided
common ground with Eoin, who listened and talked endlessly
on all that happened between our meetings.

The owner of the tent allowed me to take it one week-end
by myself. My thoughts flew to Eoin, for he had promised to
let me pitch camp in their orchard. It would possess special

marvels now that high summer's splendours heightened into autumn. The bright sun mellowed, looms of gossamer caught and held it as, hung with drops of dew, they spanned newly blossomed ling and lady's thimble.

With the tent bundled under my arm I ran towards Eoin when the lorry had set me down, and all the bells of heaven were clashing in my ears. We passed our day as usual and then Eoin left me to go into the town.

I floated in a continuum of delight, enchanted by the autumnal tang among the gnarled apple trees. My practised eye found a flat stretch of grass and then the tent stood taut, and I lay inside, an exercise book open, a stub of pencil in my mouth, my diary and nature notes of the day completed.

Now the secret night began its work and urgent owls swooped about. I mused on all that we would do to-morrow. Then from across the meadows, quite distinct from the low, recurrent *tu-whit tu-whoo*, I heard the rain. At the beginning it merely caressed the earth. The first drops patted the canvas over my head. It changed to a steady downpour and a chorus of runnels began.

I sat up, wondering if the roof would leak, or if a river would suddenly appear under my blankets. And at last the thunder rumbled up like distant wagons, and burst in savage rending claps above me. In the lightning I saw the tent-pole silhouetted and through a crack in the entrance flaps, apple branches twisted in agonized gestures under a livid sky. Then Eoin was there, crouched in the doorway. He made me dress and put a sack round my shoulders and took me down to the cottage.

Eoin's step-sister, Bridget, took a fancy for me, and insisted on teaching me to dance, as her brother had insisted on my learning to swim. They made me feel happy and secure, despite a little red lamp flickering before a holy picture in the kitchen. The sense of safety even survived after I discovered

Lough Neagh Summer

Eoin's rosary under his pillow—the Devil's Beads. The chunky walls and tiny windows of their home and its wide, open hearth, black pots and peat fire, was my dream of a wild country cottage come true.

On a table in the corner stood Bridget's proud possession— a wind-up gramophone crested by a green horn that curved magnificently upwards like a giant Robin-run-the-hedge. From the dark bend in its throat foxtrots and waltzes spat out with an odd, hissing, unworldly sound.

Delighted to have someone from Belfast who could get records, Bridget entrusted me with what seemed large sums of money. I had to go into Smithfield for her and hunt out the latest music. This task I undertook willingly, for Smithfield second-hand market was a treasure house, where hours or days could be whiled away among the precious oddments tossed up on the crest of the wave by the constantly changing fortunes of our city.

A visit to Smithfield could become a pilgrimage, a sort of homage to the multifarious facets of the human mind. With no obligation to buy, you could wander round the glass-roofed aisles or in and out of the shops, bemused by mountains of books, antiques, paintings, shops with rows and heaps of keys or mechanical parts, others with stacks of music sheets or leaning towers of records, old clothes depots and furniture dealers, cameras and carpets, bicycles and all the bibelots in my room at home. The old collector of Chinese *objets d'art* had given me many things, and round this elegant core I had built up a collection of curios derived, through jumble sales, from the Arabian Nights Smithfield.

Bridget treated me in the same way as Eoin, and indeed the whole family, as if I were grown-up. They accepted me, as though the manly qualities I craved were mine already. And the first mail I ever received came from Bridget. When the postman pushed open the letter-box and a postcard, with my name on it, flipped to the floor, I knew no way to express my joy. The postman's knock was rare enough at our house, I could remember deliveries only twice before. First with the telegram about my father's death in the 'hospital', and then with a letter for Big 'Ina. A sailor admirer had written it and no doubt would have skinned me alive, had he known that I took his love note to school to display the sentiments he had couched in no uncertain way.

Alike in kindness and friendship to me, Bridget and Eoin differed in other respects. The gentle fisherman with his slow speech and dark complexion seemed overshadowed in the house by his vivacious sister, who tossed her flaxen hair as she laughed. I loved the cottage so much, and thought that nothing could ever undermine its stout walls, or extinguish the peat fire. But one day, later in the year, Eoin told me that Bridget had gone away to be a nun. The old fears about Mickeys clouded my mind. Visions came to me of the evil priest dancing in front of her, the razor glinting in his hand with which he would slash at her beautiful hair until it lay like swaths of corn on the floor about her.

She did not altogether vanish from the land of the living, for after a little time Eoin gave me a religious medal from Bridget. Was it possible that the lively Bridget still thought about me from behind the convent's bars and bolts? Yet the medal steadily burning a hole in my pocket proved this to be. Even though it came from her, I could not take the piece of popery into our good Orange household in case it made the roof fall in or brought the sleeping-sickness upon us all. But I could not part with the medal either, and so kept it in my safe, buried pirate-style among the sally-bushes of the railway.

Whenever I went to see Eoin, I fetched the round disc from its hiding place, and pinned it on my lapel where he would see it and be pleased. Clinging about the Madonna and Child, like clouds to the mountain, was a strong appeal, a symbol of feelings I cherished for my own mother. Somehow the air of protection and concern of a Madonna towards the Child was terribly like Big 'Ina's struggles, and her unfailing efforts to keep us out of trouble, or orphanages, and the grave. And although our preachers thumbed great Bibles and shouted hysterically that Mary's 'easy' ladder to heaven in fact led to hell and the burning lake, I could not think of her as anything other than very human and warm. Her soft face, always lighted by a rapturous expression, the gentle pose, even the soft, enfolding clothes seemed preferable to our Protestant heroes. Fine though Billy King on his charger might be, or however handsome the periwigs and lace portrayed on the Orange banners, the savage element in them was but cold comfort. But Mary, so near to our kind of life, I could well imagine bending over the tinker's fire, warming a sup of milk for 'wee Jaysus'.

Bridget moved to a convent near Belfast, and when I saw nuns walking by twos through the city I would sidle close and peer under the black and white canopy that hid their faces, hoping that one would be Bridget. Care had to be taken that none of my family, or anyone in our street saw me daring to approach such a sinister apparition.

Bridget's disappearance, as though she had been swept away in an invisible flood, pre-occupied my mind for years. Why had she gone? When I had grown old enough to forget her, I remembered her still and wrote,

> *Your little feet*
> *That tangoed to morn,*
> *And pedalled up Church Bray*
> *Twice a day,*
> *Will tango no more.*

Lough Neagh Summer

And the golden lion hair
That ate men's hearts
Will be caught and caged
Behind the white bars
Of stiff coif starch.

But the boys at the corner
Whose eyes went with you to and fro
Won't lose their heads
Because you have gone.

A little of the tough hides
Will creep after you
As cypress-like
You sweep the cloister sun.

Class Distinction

The amazing thing about Coughdrop was that she liked the radiators. In this she showed herself to be human. Accusations that I felt admiration towards anyone among the ranks of schoolteachers could never be laid against me, my friends knew me too well for that. Yet for Coughdrop, a sneaking regard hovered somewhere in my usually hostile breast. Her real name was Miss Nellie Ellmire, but the nickname had been substituted long before I slunk to a desk at the back of the form over which she was to preside. The morning was a bright September one, and I did not take kindly to the enforced desertion of the countryside and the gang's company which the new term meant. I was ten years old now, and had changed to a new, big school.

Coughdrop, however, soon vindicated her nickname and stimulated enough amusement so that for a while I could forget the Bog Meadows and the gang's wild caprices along the railway lines. She had been well named, for despite the warm, sunny weather she constantly dipped into a tin of cough lozenges. Weak bronchial tubes were also indicated by a bright orange nest of wadding which peeped above the neckline of her dress. When empty, the coughdrop tins were awarded to her favourites for pen-nibs and pencil stubs to be stored in. But lozenges and wadding together were of small avail. Poor Coughdrop did bark so. She would be seized all at once, and her rather beautiful *couleur-de-rose* changed to common beetroot. Helpless and pitiless we looked on, hoping against desperate hope that it would choke her, or at least overcome her, so that retirement to the staff-room for recovery would be necessary, so allowing us a few glorious moments of freedom. We might even have wished her death from the cough had we not known full well the lightning speed with which the school authorities would have found a replacement.

And in winter, when the wadding appeared more frequently, Coughdrop sat on the radiator—an unprecedented indulgence in my experience of schoolteachers. My previous ones in the church school had whacked us if we so much as ventured near the hot pipes. There was one in particular whose idea of hygiene was to throw open the windows on the most bitter day imaginable, line us up in front of them and conduct inhaling exercises. Bitch.

Coughdrop was humane and loved a fug. Even so, we were not allowed to hibernate—she remained, when all was said and done, a schoolteacher, which put her beyond our pale. Had she not been a good wielder of the cane her job might have been forfeit. Parents judged teachers' merits by their frequency and efficiency in using the cane, the bigger and bloodier the weals on their offsprings' hands the better the teacher. On the only occasion when my mother discovered that I had been mitching she took me to school and was not satisfied until she saw the headmaster deliver justice with his stick there and then.

Youthful freshness clung to the Coughdrop, she was the least moth-eaten of any teacher I had yet experienced. Decayed, lean or fat, or merely epileptic, most of the others had seemed ancient to my infant eyes. But such infirmities did not prevent surprising energy and agility when seizing on an unfortunate child, and dragging him to the front by arm or ear, and belabouring any exposed part of the body within reach of the flailing stick.

Students came once a year for two weeks and they, by divine ordinance, had no sticks. Therefore on them were visited all the sins of their older and qualified colleagues, and visited with vengeance. They entered their period of practical training in meekness and left usually much wiser, harder men and women. Some, no doubt, suffered greatly, and others, their illusions shattered, probably denied their calling and went into commerce or ran away to sea.

One such young man of a bird-like demeanour, pale of face, lank and yellow of hair, was one day reduced to the brink of tears. All the fight had gone out of him, though, to be sure, he was facing single-handed not only the hate and resentment we held against our ordinary teachers, but generations of such perversion and parody of the pedagogic life. His immediate concern was that our bedlam would bring the headmaster's wrath and consequent failure in examinations on his head. So he resorted to bribery and bought our silence and good behaviour by giving out sweets and chocolates. With such fodder we willingly surrendered the fragments of balloon used for making rude noises, and passed a hat round to collect up the pieces of his bicycle we had dismantled. Dizzy Murray, who shared the two-seater desk in the back row with me, went out to the playing field and retrieved the handle-bars from the top of a tall tree.

Coughdrop's régime did not entirely depend on the cane, though she used it. In itself her voice, deep and brittle, was enough to quell even the biggest thug. During parsing and general analysis, the great obsession of her life, she found that the cane helped dissection of the sentences. People like Dizzy Murray required additional aids to enable them to discover which in the sentence 'Slowly and sadly we laid him down', was the predicate. If lucky, he would draw a red chalk line under the correct part. Buck Wright was not often so lucky. Standing at the front, distinguished by his protruding teeth which seemed to fly in all directions at once, and the undeveloped arm which terrified the girls, he would hesitantly draw a blue chalk line, when asked to single out the subject. First a trembling line would appear under 'Slowly'. The cane would give a warning, resounding thwack on the blackboard. Buck would wet his finger and remove the line, while Coughdrop's face changed to a deeper red.

'Is there no duster, you idiot?' and she would fling the duster at him on the point of her stick. Poor Buck would then move along in desperation to the next word and begin to underline 'sadly'. The smouldering fire went up, Coughdrop ran amok, and only a burst of coughing saved Buck from butchery.

Of ubiquitous talent, Coughdrop took us in every subject except music, science and geometry. For each of these subjects thirty minutes each was allotted in one week. There was not, as I recall, anything particularly musical, scientific, or geometric about any of them.

The music merchant was tiny and exceptionally bandy-legged and was called The Jockey! She possessed a car and by a modicum of popularity always had enough sycophants waiting at four-thirty in the afternoons to push and get it started. The Jockey gave her lessons in the big assembly hall which, in my whole time at the school, was only used twice for its proper function—first for a performance of *Snow White and the Seven Dwarfs*, and second for a mass gas-mask demonstration, when poor Coughdrop, choking and pawing like a monkey at her mask, had to be carried out.

A piano stood on the stage of the assembly hall and we were grouped on the floor according to our height. Punctuality not being one of The Jockey's characteristics, by the time she collected us from our classroom, marched us to the hall and ranged us around her, a third of the half-hour was gone. In two years we learnt 'The Ash Grove', 'My Bonnie Lies Over the Ocean', and 'Drink to me Only'.

Music, like all else under the system, formed yet one more ordeal, especially for the shy and timid. Each of us was obliged to sing a verse of the song in question, whether we possessed a musical ear or no. The powers that be had decided music we would have, even if it had to be forced down, or up, our throats like bitter medicine. If a boy hesitated from nervousness he roused anger in The Jockey, and if high treble or squeaky he roused catcalls from us. The Jockey, deeming it her duty to extract some noise from us, if only a cry of pain, would then, like all jockeys, apply her whip.

Tears were not uncommon. No virtue attached to the boy who never wept when his frozen hands were beaten. How the cruel blood rushed boiling to the cane's weal, gripping, like red-hot irons, the broken surface of chilblains. Sometimes in prolonged cold weather, the pain was so intense that a boy would dance and scream even after the first stroke. But this would not prevent the teacher from gripping the victim's wrist and striking again and again until the punishment was ended. This official, approved torture was often inflicted because we did not hold our pens properly, usually because our hands were too cold to do so. Being caned, we were even more incapable—though such a simple deduction was beyond the wit of our educators.

Sometimes a hero would rise up amongst us, a champion of our cause. Then there would be red-letter days like that on which Lyttle Nayland, boldest of the bold, grabbed the cane and cracked it in pieces before Coughdrop could get at him. When female staff were involved in such 'back-cheek', the culprit was taken with no further ado to the room of god-almighty himself who, rightly, was judged the school's best flagellist. With one hand tattooed in masonic emblems the headmaster would hold the captive and slaughter with the other. Fortunately for me the truancy episode caused the sole visit I ever made to this sanctum.

Lyttle's master performance resulted as naturally as night followed day, in a visit to the headmaster's room, though his well-accustomed palms and bottom probably felt none the worse for the punishment. As lunch-time followed almost immediately Coughdrop decided to pay a call on Lyttle's parents. She could not believe that the yoke of slavery had been thrown off, that a symbolic cry for freedom had been made. The wrath of Lyttle's parents should be added to that of the education system.

The news of Coughdrop's intention spread in no time through the whole school. As she hurried along the street hundreds of children ran a parallel course through the entries. When she got to the house a press of children waited at one end, giving vent to a catcalling such as those narrow brick alleys never heard before or since. The failure of anyone to answer her repeated knockings seemed to us like the act of a far too patient God. Coughdrop's steps had to be retraced ignominiously amid the renewed chorusings of hidden tormentors—'Watch out, Nellie, your left leg's catching up with your right!'—'Like a lick o' me brandy-balls, missus?' —'Looking for a man, lovely?', the whole counterpoint constructed over a ground bass of 'Nellie Ellmire pee'd on the fire'.

Steelworks Kelly's ma was the only parent whom I ever saw ride out to do battle with Coughdrop. A remarkable specimen indeed was Steelworks himself, altogether the most odd in the form. Tiny in stature, he could fight like a tiger. Personally I would do anything rather than get involved with him, for his skin seemed proof against fists and was like a tortoise's and not infrequently scaly with eczema. Kelly earned his name of Steelworks because his father, who followed a shoemaker's calling, once had an operation to remove thirty-five nails from his inside. In our illogical fashion we concluded that the son must have internal nails also, to cause such a leathery skin. He sat immediately in front of me, sharing his desk and immoralities with Lyttle Nayland. I hated looking at Steelwork's hair, already thin, and silky like thistledown, and coated with showers of dandruff.

The Steelworks also enjoyed notoriety because of his braces. They had animals on them and apart from fighting him it was great amusement to stretch the elastic and make the animals put on terrifying faces. In the summer, blessed summer that came to relieve our winter sufferings and brought a promise of long holidays and freedom, in those warm months we would sit in the classroom with shirt-sleeves and braces. And on the fateful day Coughdrop seized Steelworks Kelly by the back of his fancy animal ones in a moment of exasperation, and they broke in her hand.

Next morning Steelworks announced that his mother was coming up to 'do' Coughdrop. At last a David was risen up to conquer our Goliath. Even less attention than usual could be given to the lesson, we were all in a tense state waiting for Mrs. Kelly's advent. 'When's yer ma comin'?' passed to and fro in fearsome whispers. As the minutes passed we began to doubt, though ears were strained for a footfall in the corridor. And then the door was thrown open and the voice of God was heard stentoriously to say, 'Come out here where I can git at ya'.

Coughdrop flushed to boiled beetroot and strode across to the door. Mrs Kelly was now revealed bristling with curlers and with her sleeves rolled up. She had decided on the quadrangle as being the best arena in which to knock Coughdrop's block off. But her shouting, and the terror she struck were her undoing, for now the whole school roused from the dreary murmur of learning. Windows flew up, doors flew open, and other members of staff, taking in the situation in a twinkling, poured out to Coughdrop's assistance. Mrs. Kelly, struggling and demanding 'Let me at her', was driven off her prey and finally edged in the direction of the headmaster's study. A peace conference was held, as a result of which Coughdrop returned to us without a hair of her head turned. Our bitter disappointment was only slightly ameliorated when she had to buy Steelworks Kelly new braces with animals up and down each side.

In Miss Broadhouse, ostensibly dedicated to the art of geometry, unusual interest was reposited. She, according both to popular rumour and observed fact, was keen on Wally Tepping. Across the other side of the quadrangle he presided as master of the senior form, a more than ordinary man, for repute held him to be a divorcee. Straightaway, in our eyes, this set him among the socially *élite*, raised him to royal heights, for apart from Henry VIII and Mrs. Simpson we had never heard of anyone else getting divorced. By all accounts Wally Tepping must have been a wealthy man, we thought.

Miss Broadhouse's geometry classes occupied the first period on Wednesday mornings and since the register had to be marked during this time the amount of geometry we absorbed amounted to not much. And because out of thirty-five boys in our class only about four could boast pairs of compasses, our progress in Euclid's realm suffered further hindrance. Co-educational in name though our school was, in practice the girls were segregated into their own classes, and in our own, therefore, certain behaviour obtained which otherwise might have been inhibited. We stuck the points of the four compasses soundly into each other's buttocks. This lively, mirth-producing sport would doubtlessly have grown entirely out of control except for the dearth of compasses.

Such injections left Miss Broadhouse undisturbed, for

throughout the lesson one of her eyes was fixed permanently on the room across the quadrangle where a glimpse of Wally would more than compensate our lack of interest in equal or unequal angles.

This quadrangle, reserved as circulation space for the staff only, seemed dedicated to Cupid. Hordes of dogs proceeded to canine orgies encouraged by our cheers, and it was not a rarity to witness an occurrence of the most embarrassing order when the fire-buckets of stagnant water were brought into play.

We lost nothing by the quadrangle being staff-only territory because we had the field to play in. A screen of tall willows fringed one end of it and the other rose in a steep incline left wild with uncut grass. And here it was we fought. Certainly none of us could remember what place we held in class with regard to spelling or arithmetic, but we never forgot our position on the fighting championship ladder. He who stood on the top rung kept his position by his fists. Under this system everybody eventually fought everybody, the weak and fearful being more than content to remain so, the strong consumed with ambition to be the school's prize fighter.

Two black eyes which I received, swollen and purple like ripe plums, alarmed my mother, for I looked out on the world from two narrow slits into which even a penny on edge would not have fitted. Such bruises did not usually frighten Big 'Ina. Having got two herself from my father on the day Helen was born, she had to escape to the public park. The fear that seized her because of my exaggerated Chinese slits was blindness. Our clan had more than its share of that already.

I gloried in my battle wounds, however, because they had earned me fifth place in our pugilistic roll. Cecil Martin, my opponent, though not marked so visibly as myself, was pronounced defeated because he stayed away from school the next day.

After the death of my cousin Capstack the field would occasionally lose its attraction. I could sense death and his ever-ready scythe lurking among the willows. And Uncle John's voice lingered in my ears, the hollow, void voice that described the bruises which marked his son's sad little body as he undressed him for the coffin—fatal blows delivered on the playground.

I did not want to be dead like Capstack. The sharp distinction between being alive and not being alive suddenly became clear to me. The vague theories of returning to the world in the form of birds still remained. But now I saw my life and death in a more practical, realistic light, and the fact that it would affect others beside myself became clear.

I would not like my mother's voice to speak emptily over my body. Besides, now that my growing-up accelerated, I had already heard the note of pleasure creeping in when she declared to the neighbours that one day I would be big enough 'to make a peeler'. This, I knew, was her way of expressing pride in my stature. No doubt she kept in mind the early years when so often it was touch-and-go whether I would survive at all. Although my mother might consider me big enough for a prospective peeler, she certainly had no intentions of my becoming a policeman. Oh, no, her concern was that I should 'serve my time'; she had already conferred with an old admirer who promised to get me a shipyard apprenticeship. To what use then could I put the sloppy letters written in class during composition in answer to imaginary 'Smart Lad Wanted' advertisements? Too much poverty in her own life, too many relations unemployed, had made my mother determined that no such fate should befall me. I must not be an unskilled labourer but 'have my yard trade at the back of me'.

Class Distinction

Now that every month seemed to add noticeably to my height and the food I devoured appeared at last to be showing results in terms of muscle and bone, and even the jaunts to the country bleached the ecru of my face and dyed roses into my cheeks, my mother could allow herself a dream. Her goal was to have a man in the house again—and a man with his trade behind him. No, of all times I could not afford to die now. Inwardly the new resolution to keep my body in safety pleased me, for at heart I was a coward. I swung my fists in fury and without style, summing-up my opponent's capacities before fighting and as far as possible avoiding the brutes heftier than myself. Capstack's poor body covered with the bullies' bruises was the writing on the wall, it came before me a hundred times on the playground. My abstinence was translated as cowardice pure and simple. I was called a 'yella bugger'. Then I threw shipyard and apprenticeship and the vision of Capstack to the winds, and in the rush of temper would follow the old, familiar thud of knuckle on muscle, and the din and roar of blood.

As we were co-educational the girls also used our field and were by no means exempt from our attentions. Growing tired of fighting we turned to pulling their plaits to an accompaniment of 'ding-dong' sung in a metallic voice to imitate the sharp bell on the trams. The girls screamed and made a great fuss about having their hair used as a bell-cord, but I noticed that the less popular ones always lurked near, hoping to be included in the rape of innocence. The bolder, tougher ones would round on their attackers with an unladylike, 'I'll bloody well do ya'.

Our attitude to the girls changed somewhat on Friday afternoons, when we became solicitous and as polite as we knew how, for then they bore home the results of their cookery class. But the tasty things which favouritism won from the fair sex were often rudely snatched by bullies who, unlucky themselves, wanted a look-in on apple-pie or hot scones.

Love smiled kindly on me, when I was older, in the form of one Maureen Rodgers who had replaced Minnie Moore of church school fame. A Friday banquet that has not evaporated from memory was one Maureen gave me on the waste land lying between the river and the school. The winter afternoon light drained from the sky as we tucked into cauliflower *au gratin*. Until that day cheese dishes were anathema to me, but now became a special relish. After the cauliflower episode I kept Maureen's handkerchief under my pillow, but only because I thought it romantic and knew she would ask me what I had done with it.

Apart from the amusements which we organized for ourselves, the school field saw no 'organized games' though it could boast a football pitch somewhere between grass and mud. The staff included no games master and each teacher had consequently to conduct his or her own class for gym in the assembly hall. Gym appealed to us but not to Coughdrop, for not only did cold draughts haunt the hall, but she had to perch on the platform to give us practical examples of hands-forward-swing, knees-full-bend and all the rest of the physical culture repertoire. Her sturdy legs and flopping breasts seen in such untoward actions had a hypnotic effect on us.

'Do this—do that' was the only game taught us. In various states of undress (we had no gym shorts or any fancy equipment of that sort) we stood around, hanging on Coughdrop's every move and word. If she raised her arms or bent her knees and snapped 'Do *this*' then we must do it also. But if she touched her toes or swung her trunk and said 'Do *that*', and we did it, then we would have to retire from the game. As the game progressed and one by one we dropped out for failing to recognize the fatal *that*, Coughdrop would gather speed like a runaway cart on a hill, and almost explode with exertion as 'Do this! Do that' burst out to the accompaniment of her weird jerky movements.

We imbibed science, in the week's best period, from Miss Cartright, a lady who, like her musical colleague, could never be punctual. Nature endowed her generously with a moustache. While kept waiting in the cold corridor we would say a dozen times, not too audibly, 'Come on Ma Cartright, finish yer shavin'.'

Age determined the prefix 'Ma', as next to the headmaster she was the oldest member of staff. No make-up or powder concealed the network of fine lines that crinkled her face like a dried-up apple. I held her in special favour because out of the entire staff she was the only one ever to contribute anything to my pin-hole card—a hard circumstance I thought in view of the widespread belief that schoolteachers were 'rotten' with money.

With mounting anticipation I longed for lunch-time to come and the knocking on the staffroom door. The blue card was taken in, and the teachers looked at it as if obscenities were printed on it. They passed it on, and so on, right round the room until Wally Tepping handed it back to me and said, 'Scram'.

But Miss Cartright made atonement. As I walked crestfallen along the corridor to the playing field I spied her working alone in the laboratory. Perhaps some chord of remembered sympathy still vibrated, for I plucked up courage and presented the card to her. She listened carefully as I explained the pin-hole system and she studied the card. I came away two pennies the richer.

Science classes enjoyed their popularity because they provided a greater variety of things for us to play with than any other. They also meant an interesting assortment of objects for us to take home for private experiments though the school authorities would have referred to this as stealing. The most self-righteous could not resist helping themselves to a yard of the glass tubing which made such perfect pea-shooters or could be bent over a gas-oven's flame into such splendid shapes.

And for science as such, or rather as Ma Cartright showed it to be, we were all eyes and ears. When she put a match to her Bunsen burner and adjusted its serrated collar to tame the flame or make it fierce, she led us into new regions. It was the world of true romance, where reality denied itself and the invisible became visible. Miss Cartright did not just talk like all the others, she actually did things. Her laboratory seemed imbued with as much mystery as those in woodcuts of medieval alchemists, where curious ingredients steam in queer-shaped pots and a bat or two hovers in the corner.

Miss Cartright, we thought inarticulately, prised open the secrets of the universe as a gourmet might flick oysters open. Indeed, she did in a way, but not with chemicals or electricity so much as with our young minds. She, more than anyone, roused our curiosity and wonder, so laying in us the beginning of wisdom.

Bunsen burner blazing, Miss Cartright would get the special key for the cupboard with the dangerous phosphorus, carefully cut a small piece and put it in a crucible. Then, locking the cupboard, she would walk to the demonstrating table as if carrying a hydrogen bomb. And as she floated the crucible on water, lit the phosphorus, and placed a glass bell on top, so that the oxygen inside should burn up, we all sat tensed, waiting, hoping for an explosion that never came.

On occasions like these, rather than allow the arbitrary timing of the period to cut short the drama of discovery, a plot was laid. The science-room stood apart from the main school buildings and was warned of lesson change-overs by an electric bell. Two of us would ask to be 'excused please, Miss', when the period's end drew near, and would muffle the bell when it began to ring. The extra quarter hour so gained in Miss Cartright's room would then be terminated only when an urgent message by hand arrived to say that another class was waiting.

Music. Science. Geometry. To this trinity of topics which took us away from the Coughdrop's eagle eye was added an occasional period of religion. The care of the seven episcopalian souls in our class was given over to an elderly clergyman. Coughdrop was a Presbyterian black-mouth and therefore in no position to direct our salvation. While the seven of us joined boys from other classes and crowded into the room devoted to the scripture lesson, Coughdrop would supervise her fellow black-mouths elsewhere.

If the science classes afforded us a maximum of interest, the scripture ones provided the greatest entertainment. This was in no way due to the cleric's attempts to make plain the profound mysteries which, we all agreed, comprised the Book of Common Prayer. It was rather due to the fact that our tutor was partially deaf and, more importantly, came to us quite unarmed. He brought no weapon against us, not so much as an umbrella. This put him at once to disadvantage and often on his way home he must have been tempted to think that not all peacemakers are blessed. But even equipped in the normal manner with a cane, he would have found difficulty in controlling the class, for we sat cramped three and sometimes four in a desk intended for two, and this, of course, added to our fun.

Our preceptor was very bald on top and the fringe of hair round it fascinated me and obviously did him also. The white tonsure was allowed to grow extremely long and was then well oiled, and swept upwards like a wave turning itself over on the shore, in an attempt to cover the naked summit of his head. Coming up the path one frosty morning he slipped on the ice and the careful coiffure fell asunder. He arrived in the school looking like a scarecrow with hair of straw. But more intriguing than his hair was the little silk vest under the clerical collar. As he straightened himself the black triangle stuck out from his waistcoat. I was surprised to see it was only a tiny bib and not the special priestly shirt I imagined it to be. For me it amounted to deception and reduced his sanctity. It was like Great-Grandfather Dick preparing for the Twelfth of July and my seeing the ninety-year-old bag of bones with a paper dickie on the naked breast while two starched cuffs decorated the long, thin arms as though a wasting prisoner in gyves.

Paradoxically we gleaned more of our glorious Protestant heritage from Coughdrop than from the clergyman, for she taught us history. This meant *Foxe's Book of Martyrs*, that and nothing else. As the school owned only one copy Coughdrop used it herself, reading it aloud to us.

History periods consequently were peaceful and relatively safe for day-dreaming. I could escape. In the twinkling of an eye I could leave the smells of caked jerseys and soaked feet; the rumblings of hot pipes and the monotone of other forms' multiplication tables. I exchanged sordid necessity for life's real purposes—the running free amongst the heather and the stooping for blaeberries.

What to me were Coughdrop's martyrs shouting Protestant slogans from the stake, when I knew that tomorrow I would mitch and maybe get to a horse fair up the country? Then I would be with real Mickeys, Catholics of flesh and blood, men who ate boxty and chewed their blocks of 'War Horse'. I did not want to hear about Cranmer putting 'this unworthy hand' into the flames first. His deed was too distant and wholly removed from my new life of roads where hearty red-faced farmers spat on their hardened, knobbly hands, and brought them smacking down on a neighbour's to clinch a cattle deal.

Class Distinction

True, such dreams were apt to be sawn in half by a swish of the cane. As it cut an arc by my ear I would be conscious of a ridiculous command, perhaps 'Describe Latimer's last act!' With the dream lying shattered around me, the hot feeling in my stomach swelled as my confusion covered me. No doubt about the next inevitable step—'Hold it steady . . . steady, boy', and my hand received the reward of dreamers and the effect caused Coughdrop to begin croaking.

Failure to record the only two things Coughdrop taught me for which I felt gratitude would leave too dismal a picture of her, though admittedly they were hardly scholastic attainments. The first was how to eat my food. Since the school lay a good distance from home I had to take my 'piece', and devoured it at midday in company with several others. We sat on at our desks when everyone else had gone home and unwrapped our packages. Coughdrop ate her cheese and celery which I fetched from the Maypole. In our anxiety to get out the food would be bolted down in as large pieces as gullets would allow and in an entirely unmasticated state. Coughdrop had contrary ideas. 'You're not pigs altogether!' she would shout, whirling the stick. Then, solemnly, she would time the devouring of each mouthful, and in the end I began to enjoy this leisurely habit. And useless was the attempt to bolt the remainder when she stopped the timing and returned to her newspaper, for we thought she had pinholes pierced in the paper so that she could watch us.

The second habit learnt from Coughdrop was care of my hair. Until she took the situation in hand I had gone about with my straight fine hair hanging over my eyes in a donkey fringe. When the other boys and I joined her form, by a double process of direct insistence and subtle suggestions that we were no longer babies, she got us to drive a parting through our hair and to belabour it with a brush. My mother willingly bought a wire brush that looked as if intended for terriers' backs, and I soon had my locks glistening in their own natural oil, and lying as flat as a pancake. The method and style long outlived any satisfaction it gave Coughdrop.

Untidy hair was accorded only a mild rebuke compared with that given for the nasal performance of what we called 'snot-chords'. It being too much to expect that we should carry handkerchiefs, this prolonged hawking resulted in our being peremptorily dispatched to the lavatory.

Similarly cleanliness obsessed her, at least *we* considered it an obsession. Woe to him on whose fingers Nellie detected the stains of nicotine! Tide-marks on boys' necks received no quarter, home he was sent to remove it and be punished on his return. This particular evil never befell me for my mother always made certain to see we never 'cow-licked' and equally she frequently 'bug-raked' our heads. Shame indeed would it have been to her if a school medical inspection revealed a colony of the 'wee men'.

Our chief weapon against Coughdrop's onslaughts of hygiene was the farting. This habit, probably engendered in the first instance by a poor diet, could be exaggerated at will, and the result was to drive poor Coughdrop to the edge of apoplexy. More irate than on any other occasion she would demand to know which of us wanted to 'go'. Ability in 'blowing' was an achievement scarcely to be ranked below skill with fists. And a favourite form of torment given to jinnies in the playground was to snatch their hands, hold them over our rumps, and invite them as crudely as we knew how to 'catch this!'

Measures of a more positive nature which could be undertaken against Coughdrop included the emasculation of the cane. Should any of us happen on the classroom and find it empty then we knew our duty, a knowledge with which we seemed to have been born. Hiding or stealing the cane achieved nothing, for Coughdrop simply went off to the headmaster to get another. And in that torture chamber we believed a huge bath was let into the floor where hundreds of canes soaked in paraffin, a kind of curing process which gave them better stinging properties.

The method we used was a form of psychological warfare. Finding the classroom empty we seized the cane and a razor blade and cut the stick almost through. Then, later, when Coughdrop banged it on the desk or over someone's head, the cane bent weakly at right-angles, making her look exceedingly foolish. We could afford to laugh then.

Taking an all-round view of the bad old days in education, I did not fare too badly from Coughdrop. Towards my constant absences she bore sympathy, believing many more to have legitimate medical reasons than had in fact. She never realized that some were for visits to the clinic and the many others were for mitching to go into the country. Perhaps her own faulty chest and breathing made her understanding of my bad health. And she did not want to make too great an enemy of me for I served a useful purpose as postman. Her great woman friend taught in a school near my house, and I had often to carry letters between them, back and forth.

And of all the sorry tale, learning comes limping in at the last. Only at arithmetic and algebra did I shine, going into eclipse over English, principally because of a built-in inability to spell. I so often shared the lowest position in the class for this intractable subject with Freddy Wells, a real dafty who enjoyed our friendship solely because his mother ran a stall in the market and he always came to school well loaded.

Usually I walked home with four other boys and between us we could muster enough talent to make good individual deficiencies. On most days we called in at an old carpenter's shop, where among warm drifts of shavings we were allowed

Class Distinction

to sit on the floor and apply ourselves to the homework queries.

The genius in the king's language would work out the parsing and 'opposite words', while I wrestled with seven horses eating three loads of hay in fourteen months, and tried to find out how long it would take twelve horses to eat five loads.

In the comfortable wood loft we settled to work, perhaps the only work of that day. The carpenter was old and benevolent, and his wreath of grey curls was hung with stray shavings, and the hairy fuzz of his brown arms was sprayed with sawdust. The smell of wood and the atmosphere of the ancient craft created an incense in the place that made it holy to us in a way that the ugly school buildings would never be. The carpenter rarely spoke and took our presence for granted, except when we became too boisterous. 'Now, now, lads,' he would say, and this had more power over us than any of the day's flagellations.

Afterwards, the mathematical horses foddered, I ran home, and with my satchel roped together, threw it up the hallway and then climbed over the palings and barbed wire to find the gang and wider horizons of the sally-bushes.

Last Song

And now, with swifts already gone, swallows and martins waited in concourse to follow them south. As they settled on fences and spread along telegraph wires, autumn settled slowly over the landscape. The allan hawk arrived. Round the coasts and by inland waters all over Ulster, the red-throated diver usurped the fickle birds of summer. The appearance of winter visitors brought reminders of the scudding rain-clouds, high winds and sharp mornings to come.

On that particular Sunday we hardly noticed the miracles of migration happening around us. The flask of tea and its little frill of paper round the cork, leaned drunkenly against a tuft of grass, and I was the only one who had eaten any of the baps. Mrs. McClellan twisted the rings on her fingers and tried to suppress occasional sobs. A damp lace hanky lay crumpled on her lap.

No wonder she whimpered and could pay no attention to the birds or the tea. Mr. Chamberlain on the radio had spoilt the Sunday dinners by telling us we were going to war with Germany. It upset the old girl and brought back, as if it was only yesterday, her two brothers. 'Fine lads' she used to say in a queer mixture of affection and frustration. They had left the Devon farm, smiling, for Flanders and never came home. Mrs. McClellan's misery, not lessened by years, surged over her in waves. I felt desperately sorry for her. But what could I do? I got on with the baps, accepting Mrs. McClellan's vehement anti-German remarks as her way of letting off steam.

Hate for Germans puzzled me. Had they not produced Martin Luther who ranked next to King Billy? The hate loomed so disproportionately large in the adult world. No doubt this hate was only one of the many queer beliefs held by grown-ups. Their inexplicable insistence on Father Christmas, for instance, was a myth I had exploded very early on. Not one of the many letters I had written to him was ever answered.

At one stage my pleading became so desperate, and I penned such a number of notes that the neighbours refused to 'lend' me any more envelopes. (Having a 'lend' of the newspaper, a match, or an envelope was our word for borrowing, carrying the implicit understanding that things so loaned would never be given back). I threw my letters to Father Christmas up the chimney, and sat back to await developments.

But the letters were not collected in the night by the old gentleman with the white beard, and simply lodged in the back of the chimney. They grew in such volume that eventually they set our chimney on fire. I never dreamed such excitement existed, as that I went through when a real fire-engine, red and brazen, drew up near our door, complete with a crew of real firemen in uniform. But when they departed, it dawned on me tragically that those pathetic notes had been written to nobody. The fact was that Santa did not come down chimneys, did not in fact exist at all. Why then should grown-ups insist so elaborately that he did?

From Father Christmas to Germans was only a short step— made by way of grown-ups' attitude to Catholics, also lacking reason it seemed to me. Not only had I friends amongst the Mickeys, but I kept Bridget's medal without catching the mange, slept in their cottage without being castrated. And nuns were no longer the fiendish hags of my earliest fears, with singed rumps from the Vatican candles, who gleaned the Belfast streets for Protestant babies to carry off, hidden under their black garb. I had seen Dizzy Murray's little brother fall from a moving breadserver's van and two nuns rush at once to carry him inside their prison gates. But he confounded us later by emerging quite safe, delighted with gifts pressed on him and quite indignant that he had not been called upon to kiss the priest's feet or to witness Bibles being burnt. There was no disputing now that nuns were just like Bridget, and I could no longer fear them.

Santa, the Mickeys, now Germans—and here my own experiences could be drawn upon also. The one kindly soul encountered beyond our immediate circle, in the whole of my childhood, was the old Chinese collector, Uncle Hughie, and he was half German. Hate him? No, that would be impossible.

Sitting with a distraught and slightly hysterical Mrs. McClellan on those cliffs, on that first day of war, September 1939, made me uncomfortable. As I worked my way through the unwanted baps, I remembered the day at Uncle Hughie's house, when instead of dismissing me with instructions to call another day with my pin-hole card he took me on to his lawn to meet his young nephew and wife—Germans. They stopped playing tennis as he beckoned, and strode over to me. A kind of divine radiance shone about their blond heads and smooth tanned limbs. Nothing was ever seen in our grey city like them. And they put out their hands when introduced and shook mine. Nobody had ever done that to me before, and this was a great compliment for obviously the young god and goddess belonged to the 'quality'.

No, Mrs. McClellan's indiscriminate hate, hate in the abstract which I could not analyse but nevertheless was aware of, could not be taken seriously. Father Christmas, the Mickeys and Germans simply affected adults in a curious way. And when the collection of scrap metal began in earnest as the war became reality, I could rouse no enthusiasm to go round with the push-carts. The thought dogged me that bombs made from it might fall on the handsome couple in tennis shorts.

But after that day on the cliffs the war slowly infiltrated our lives, trickling like water on the sides of a damp cave. Coughdrop made us take silver paper to school for the Red Cross, and that fortunately lopped five minutes or so off the first lesson. Then National Savings appeared, and made another welcome interruption in the morning routine. We were not allowed to forget the war. Gas-masks must go like dogs at our heels, and follow us everywhere. If we arrived at school without them, Coughdrop whacked us and sent us home to get them.

Martyrs burning at the stake during history lessons, now had to make elbow-room for Nazis' victims. And religious instructions never passed without some cruelty of the Germans being placarded for our edification.

The great hate, channelled by careful propaganda, swamped us, sucking everything into its maelstrom. And when I heard about the char, I forgot Uncle Hughie's family, and joined in the swim. The story was not so easy to understand, for it came from Aunt Becky, who had always been so pronounced in her hatred of the Jews. But now she told me, with considerable feeling, that some friend or relative of her niece (the despised one who had married a Jew) had gone to work as a char in a Berlin block of offices. Because of her race and faith she became a suspect of the Nazis. Then one morning putting her hands in the bucket to start washing the floors, she found it full of acid, which burned the flesh off completely.

I understood the human appeal of this story. Nazi brutality was identified with something I could understand. The story was not easy to shake off, in spite of Uncle Hughie's assurances that only Hitler's followers indulged in such things. We would not have dared to doubt the authenticity of Aunt Becky's story for fear of being thought unpatriotic, though I could not help thinking why the woman had not got her own bucket of water ready, like Big 'Ina had to.

Like everybody else, I gradually began to hate Germans, not individuals or groups, but simply Germans. Yet I disliked the whole idea of war and killing, not just because British and Germans were involved. Why did men kill one another? My desire to kill Mickeys had vanished, why should I want to kill Germans, hate them as I may, who were so far away? Nobody seemed able to answer.

My immediate concern was that when the gas-bombs dropped and we were all be-snouted with masks—what would happen to the birds? the strong-winged jenny dabbers —the throngs of starlings that made a restless aviary of the City Hall, where a bit of good luck could always be got by standing under the rows of birds—what would happen to them all? And would the spring balls of moss, where wrens poked out of the smallest hole, be turned for ever into forsaken, sodden nests, tattered and without the warmth and scent of hungry fledglings? Would all be gassed and silenced? Would January no longer ring with that eerie scream of vixen ready for her mate, and the woods of heaven echo no more with the choir of half-moons and the pavan of billing pigeons?

The matron of the poor people's holiday-home at Bangor, where Big 'Ina had taken us on our first holiday, remembered me, when I called one day with my pin-hole card. She had retired now and lived not far away from us. Entrusted with the amassing of jumble-sale material, and selling a dozen-and-one varieties of concert and social tickets besides, for the church and mission halls, I never missed her house. She did not always have oddments to give but made me welcome nevertheless, and sometimes asked me to run messages for her.

Last Song

Imperceptibly, I absorbed her attitude to the war business—that of the Society of Friends. I was almost thirteen now but she discussed affairs with me as if I were a man already. Her outlook of non-violence impressed me immensely. I felt less muddled to learn that a large body of people disapproved of killing as I did, and regarded myself as a Quaker, having first made sure that porridge eating, which I still loathed, was not involved. Becoming a Quaker had the added attraction of having a religion different from that of everyone else in our street. And now I had a new hall to visit with all the thrills of the Saturday cinema, new characters and new plots. I respected the Friends, but did not doubt that there would be as much fun as in the mission halls. And with my new status as an adult I thought, let Mr. Chamberlain fall out with Hitler, why should it matter to us? (And then reverting to my usual mode of thinking, wondered why he had not taken Hitler by that ridiculous forelock and given him a thorough 'bashing' to settle it there and then.)

And the trickle of war began to bring changes at home too. At last my pacts and appeasements with God bore results. Great-Aunt Agatha closed her house against me for ever. It all happened because the squeamish cousin Nathaniel was entrusted to my care one Twelfth of July. We went to Finaghy Field to see the meeting. With the blasting Lambeggers and the pipe-bands, the unlimited flow of porter, the holiday spirit caught everyone like flames in a barley field. Near Nathaniel and me, a woman was giving a *Folies Bergère* of her own, and providing the chief attraction. She aimed to rouse the patriotic Orangemen by kicking her ancient leg up, so that they could see her bloomers made from a Union Jack.

Forgetting Nathaniel's saintliness, I joined in the cheering and encores. Nathaniel was horrified—into silence. Not a word would he say until we reached Agatha's house again, where his tell-tale news of my wickedness exploded like a

burst dam. Immediately, a conclave was convened, and published its findings that perhaps, after all, I should be kept away.
An imminent danger they saw was that far from being
straightened out myself, I was likely to lead my cousin from
the way of salvation.

Consummate victory! When that dread front-door shut,
it never opened to me again. Shortly afterwards Agatha was
taken ill and had to go into hospital herself. Great twin ropes
of her brindle hair lay down the banks of pillow, and clasped
hands jutted out of a lawn-sleeved nightdress. I had to go and
see her.

'You've been up to something,' was her greeting before
the whole MacDonald clan.

The sleepiness about her eyes dissolved, and a hardness
developed as though she were face to face with the devil. I
really thought her clairvoyant, for on the way to the hospital
I had found two beer bottles and took them into a pub for the
penny rebate. Before she could choke her righteous soul by
trying to rebuke me further, I was taken out of the ward. 'Up
to something' were the last words to me before she passed to
her harp and forty-five wreaths—that was goodness and mercy
following you to the very grave. Aunt Becky was quick to
remark that it was even better than Mrs. Williams's, her
minister's aunt, who had been to America and had forty-two
wreaths.

When my mother next went to hospital, I was sent to
Great-Aunt Emma's. Before going Big 'Ina had told us she
was in for a 'rippin' great op'. For the first time in many
years I saw her weep on leaving us—she to whom tears did
not come easily.

But fighting all the way she pulled through, and again
we were reunited at home. The hospital had sent her home
with a solemn warning—no more heavy work. If she went
back to her old jobs . . . and here the doctor had shrugged

his shoulders. But we had to live, so we took in lodgers. The war was getting into stride, and thousands of workers were swarming into Belfast to build the great battleships of the British Navy.

Our house was small, but it had two bedrooms and the return. My bed was taken out of the back room and set up in my mother's. This left my room free for 'one double', which could hold three men. The return had no fireplace, being nothing more than a box-room, and patterns of damp had replaced the faded designs on the wallpaper. Eight feet long and five feet wide, the return was pressed into war-service too, and a bed found for it, a large single one. I felt envious of the occupants who would have the novel experience every night of climbing over the end, in order to get in. The bed was intended to hold two, but now three generally used it, and this meant up to six sometimes, when we had night-shifters, who sprawled in it by day.

Many of the return's occupants were country boys come to Belfast to work in the railway coalyards. When they came in from the yards, they were covered in coal-dust black as chimney-sweeps. And when Big 'Ina was out, perhaps defying the doctors and doing a little charring, it fell to me to make sure that the boys washed properly before falling into the beds just vacated by the other shift.

An entirely different set-up obtained in the back room. Three young musicians from the Opera House slept there. They had mysteriously managed to grow up without be-. coming set and uninteresting. I hung about the house when they were at home, enjoying the laughter they brought and the jokes that my mother joined in. A secret fund of happiness was theirs, and I loved to see them steal each other's turns at the kettle of hot water for shaving, or sit at the table drumming knives and forks, dressed in evening suits ready for the evening performance.

Last Song

Terry, the funniest and smallest, played the double-bass, humping it down our street like Bunyan's Pilgrim with his burden. For me, it ousted the fiddler's dancing bow in the entry, and instead I would have private parlour concerts, while Terry practised, running through endless variations, without once looking at music. Twelve inches above his black spaniel hair, the scroll turned on itself, like shells brought home years ago from the sands of Down. He kept the instrument in a beautiful condition, and used a silk cloth to stroke the varnish. The great back, worn shiny by generations of care, was like a glossy animal—one of the missionaries' lions sleeping under an African sun. Big 'Ina hardly knew what to make of the double-bass, and as if it really was a lion, locked the parlour door when Terry was not in the house. And I would peep through the window to make sure that nothing had happened to it.

Besides bringing the breath of a wider world into our house, the lodgers also brought a higher standard of living. We could have sausages and fried potato-bread for tea more often. This treat meant we were redeemed from the worst poverty—people who could afford sausages for tea were in comparative luxury. Helen could now sing with her friends as they whirled skipping ropes round,

> *Half a pound of sausages*
> *Frying on the pan,*
> *None for nobody else,*
> *Only me and my wee man.*

Not all our lodgers were as thoughtful as Terry, who often got out the frying-pan himself and made the tea. We had a run of bad luck with some rearing giants of men, brutes who rolled back drunk to the house, and then refused to vacate the bed when the shift coming off work arrived home. Two of them became embroiled with the police and a struggle took place as they were hustled into the black maria. Having *that* right outside our door made a change from the ambulance and gave the neighbours something to talk about over tea. And other bad characters refused to pay up their money to Big 'Ina, and after two weeks' free keep, mysteriously left.

Belfast reacted swiftly to the coming of war, its streets vibrated with energy, everyone was working—even me. After school I helped in a grocer's. From large sacks I had to weigh out flour and sugar into small bags. Not so pleasant was the shelling of rotten pods, so that the peas could be sold. But this employment was terminated rather sharply one day, when I came out of the shop with a load of eggs hidden under my lumber-jacket. They were intended as the main course of the gang's supper that night.

The shopkeeper's wife busying herself with a box of apples smiled as I passed her, 'Goin' Robbie?' Now of all times I did not want her to chat. I walked by without answering and then she called, 'Here.' My heart sank. 'Ye're covered in whitin' off the wall' she said and began to brush me down with her hand. It was too late. With one stroke she smashed some of the eggs and they began to ooze out in a yellow mess of yolks.

Enticed away by glory and the royal shilling, Gandhi left the gang with no successor. His binding power gone, the gang split into factions and became a house divided. Then the summer heat caked the verdant banks along the railway, and the grass grown long, withered away. And whether a flying spark from an engine caused it, or one of the gang's fires we never knew, but a conflagration raged through the sally-bush under-growth, devouring the grass and thickets for half a mile. An advertisement hoarding was damaged, and other property facing the banks severely singed. In the flames' wake came the police, watching and waiting for us to appear. But we had fled like animals from a forest fire. Nothing about the sally-bushes could fascinate us now, the cloistral tunnels were a black, forlorn ruin.

Now a dilemma faced me. I was lost without the gang, yet newer and weaker groups of boys had not the same attraction. Like Gandhi, all unaware I was preparing for a fuller life, and with the old ties broken, I felt no consuming desire to form new ones. The war excitement and the coming and going of lodgers at home made up for some of the loss. But I could not give my heart to these things, or be absorbed in them. I wanted something to *happen*.

And it did, pretty soon. The news was more startling than anything so far, and much more real to us than Mr. Chamberlain's Sunday broadcast. We were going to be evacuated!

The government would send us far away from Belfast to the remote west—into Fermanagh. This was fundamental, an event in my life to be put alongside all the other great events. I knew a change would take place, causing a break in the years, like the vast faults in the basalt cliffs, where you could see a dark fissure dividing rock from rock. Had not Mrs. McClellan seen the change in my teacup months before?

Long-drawn-out sighs of relief from the great-aunts greeted the news as an answer to their constant prayers. Since I was always mitching school to go out to the moors and mountains, and had filled the backyard with plants, so that everyone had to hack their way through a jungle to reach the lavatory, they thought it a highly suitable way to dispose of me. Let the government support me for the next year until I was old enough to return and work in the shipyard. They imagined their part done, particularly now Agatha was dead and could no longer terrify everyone.

Between them, they had guarded me from my father's family, sewn my pockets up, cured me of stooping by the most painful processes imaginable, and had finally stopped me from biting my nails. And to reinforce their feeling that getting rid of me was the culmination of their duties, was the fact that the tuberculosis clinic had finally discharged me, with an injunction to stay in the open-air as much as possible. With God and the government behind them, the great-aunts felt sure they were right in encouraging Big 'Ina to give her consent.

And for the first and only time in my whole life, I agreed with them. The prospect of a summer in the country, indeed a whole year, thrilled me almost more than anything I could remember. It would be like a prolonged camping session, or a life lived on the lake shores bird-watching with Eoin. Fermanagh, the unexplored lakeland of the west, became a constant dream with its forests and numerous islands.

I could hardly bear the time that dragged now. I learnt by heart the list that Coughdrop had chalked on the blackboard, of all the things that must be packed and taken on the great exodus. No second pair of shoes could be put in *my* suitcase, but that did not matter as I preferred plimsolls anyway. A lodger went off without paying, and so I got his nice blue suit left, in his anxiety to be gone, in the wardrobe. It fitted me well, and would make the perfect Sunday rig-out. Big 'Ina's idea that I should not wear long trousers until my fourteenth birthday was all very well. But already my legs, making me nearly six feet tall, looked ridiculous in the short pants bought new when I was eleven. Gradually, Coughdrop's list was crossed off, the things collected, a case borrowed from next door and my new belongings packed.

Farewells had to be said. Uncle Hughie gave me a bob and a blessing, and my Quaker friend presented a soap-bag. I decided to leave Eoin until the Saturday. On the Sunday morning I would be gone. Heaven, that through the years I had heard so much about, would have been mine indeed, if only I could have been evacuated out to Eoin's. But I knew the government would never put one of its Protestant supporters into a Mickey's house.

By Saturday, all was ready, and I got a lorry-lift out of Belfast, and walked across to Eoin's cottage. But not a trace of life showed except for hens pecking at the whitewash on the walls. I felt my stomach go hot, and my heart beat faster. I had not seen him for several weeks now, and during them another cloud of fear had drifted into my horizon. Eoin had talked about joining the army. I did not take it seriously at first, for people said scornfully that no Mickey would want to fight on behalf of a Protestant king. And would Eoin himself, kind and slow of speech, want to fight, the man of fishing nets, who had the nose of a setter for wildfowl—would he really think of leaving the most wonderful hearth in all Ireland for the barrack rooms of England?

I knocked and knocked, and heard only a hollow echo inside. I pressed my nose against every window. A gush of misery opened in me, but in the end I had to go, for the last-minute arrangements in Belfast. I had brought Eoin a packet of his favourite Pontefract liquorice, and I laid it in the side shed where the wood was neatly piled. I knew his habits of old, and was certain he would find it on coming home. Hanging on the axe's handle was Eoin's beret. How many times had I seen him in it?

Suddenly the hat seemed to be part of him. I snatched it up and buried my face in it. The smell of his hair carried me back through all our happy times together, right from the very first day when I thought he wanted to drown me. At least now, thanks to him, I would be able to swim in Fermanagh's lakes. Then I turned, and ran through the little patch in front of the cottage, scaring the hens which squawked and scurried from the path, while the bolder Rhode Island Red cock ran crossly after me.

Last Song

At home my mother was busy getting the men's early Saturday tea. She gave me a penny to get a dollop of soft brown soap, for us all to wash our hair. When the men had spruced up in their best suits and had gone off to the pubs, Big 'Ina and Cissy disappeared too. Then I got the absurd little tin bath (it would hold no more than two bucketfuls) and after Helen had come out, sat in it in front of the kitchen fire. I soaked and washed myself as never before, for now the great change in the course of life was almost on me. In a way, I was already a man, and wanted to begin as clean as a new pin. The next night I would be alone in a strange household, only the fears and loves of the old life stirring in my heart, to remind me of what was left behind.

When I had dried myself, and put a coalbrick on the fire to keep it in for Big 'Ina's return, I climbed the stairs. The house shivered from the passing trains. Because it was my last night Big 'Ina had said I could take the gas mantle out of the parlour light, and use it in the bedroom, a rare treat I had known before only in illness.

Helen and I put all the final bits and pieces into the case, and then emptied it all out again, to make sure that I had not forgotten anything. We did this a dozen times until the excitement had worn off. Then we ransacked the old marble-topped washstand, where the family heirlooms hid amongst the spare sheets and hats. For the last time I took a look at Grandfather's war medals, and opened up the Wee Lamplighter's old fishing-bag, to see all the important documents inside, including the scrappy remains of Big 'Ina's love letter from the sailor.

The gas went gently down, demanding another penny we did not have. From a sun in a morning fog, the mantle changed to a yellow daffodil and then only a smudge of amethyst and rose rubbed the white ash socket. We put the documents back, the 'weddin' lines', the birth certificates, and the title-deeds of the six-foot plot that lay on the hillside beyond the Bog Meadows and the shallow Blackstaff.

And still, in spite of all the lean and bitter years, the grave lacked its one more adult or two children.